ROGER FREESTONE
ANOTHER DAY AT THE OFFICE

Roger Freestone with his wife, Sue, and his children, Dan and Lauren.

ROGER FREESTONE
ANOTHER DAY AT THE OFFICE

KEITH HAYNES & PHIL SUMBLER

For Susan, Dan and Lauren – and of course for supporters of Swansea City everywhere.

TEMPUS

First published 2001

PUBLISHED IN THE UNITED KINGDOM BY:

Tempus Publishing Ltd
The Mill, Brimscombe Port
Stroud, Gloucestershire GL5 2QG

PUBLISHED IN THE UNITED STATES OF AMERICA BY:

Tempus Publishing Inc.
2A Cumberland Street
Charleston, SC 29401

Tempus books are available in France and Germany
from the following addresses:

Tempus Publishing Group
21 Avenue de la République
37300 Joué-lès-Tours
FRANCE

Tempus Publishing Group
Gustav-Adolf-Straße 3
99084 Erfurt
GERMANY

British Library Cataloguing in Publication Data.
A catalogue record for this book is available from the British Library.

ISBN 0 7524 2169 7

Typesetting and origination by Tempus Publishing.
PRINTED AND BOUND IN GREAT BRITAIN.

CONTENTS

FOREWORD

'Colin, we've got a goalkeeper who can go all the way.' With those words, Graham Reynolds, my then chief scout at Newport County, helped me launch the career of Roger Freestone. As usual, Graham was right; the Big Lad – all 6ft 3in of him – did make it to the highest level.

I remember meeting Roger when he came to Somerton Park with his dad for the first time as a teenager. Even at fifteen, he had the build, the ability and, of course, the potential. He was a big boy with big hands who looked the part. Graham had seen a lot of him and, after he'd played in a couple of trial games, we signed Roger as a trainee. In April 1986, he became a full-time professional and, after only 13 League appearances during the following year, he was sold to Chelsea for £95,000 – a small fortune for a club like Newport in those days.

I am so pleased that he's gone on from there and done so well. After nearly ten years with Swansea, Roger won the ultimate prize for a footballer – the chance to represent his country – when he played for Wales against Brazil at the Millennium Stadium in 2000, which was also the year the Swans created history by winning the Division Three championship for the first time. Throughout his career, Roger has been a model of consistency and professionalism and I don't think I've come across any player in all my years in the game who deserved recognition more.

It's lovely to have re-established contact with him since I've returned to League football as manager of Swansea. He's a bit of a joker who likes a laugh, but Roger also takes his job very seriously. I just hope we can keep him going for a few more years! I know he's thirty-three, but his fitness levels are very good and he's got a while to go before he reaches 'veteran' status. It's a priviledge to be asked to write the preface to the life story of such a safe pair of hands, a superb shot-stopper and, most of all, one of the genuinely nice guys in football.

Colin Addison
Swansea
October 2001

ACKNOWLEDGEMENTS

Many thanks and appreciation to the following people and establishments, without whom this book, and Roger Freestone's testimonial year, would have been that much harder to achieve. The authors thank: Gareth Keen, Glan Letheran, Frank Burrows, Ken Bates and Chelsea FC, Colin Addison, John Lewis, Steve Jones, Martin Thomas, Julian Alsop, Alan Curtis, Matthew Bound, Mickey Howard and all the players at Swansea City FC, John Hartson, Ryan Giggs, Mark Hughes, Gary Speed, David Seaman, Ceri Stennet, Jan Molby, Jon Wilsher, Paul Abbandonato, Phil Dillon, James Howarth at Tempus, Duncan Rawlings (Paperbox, Cheltenham), The Steve James Benefit Committee at Glamorgan CCC, Ivor and Sheila , Eddie & Gloria Freestone, John Freestone, Myra Powles & Joyce Butler (SCFC Club Shop), Peter Owen (Communications Officer SCFC), Jackie Rockey & Martin Burgess (SCFC), Linden Jones, Paul Compton, Sam Hammam and Cardiff City FC, Richard Jones (*Total Football*), Gary Martin, Kieron McDonnell, The Swansea City Supporters Trust, Tony Santore, Rivals.Net, Gary Thomas, our particular friends and contacts at the BBC with Welsh football at heart, Eddie Niedzwiecki, *The South Wales Evening Post*, *Western Mail* and *Wales On Sunday*, Lyn Phillips and the South Wales Police, Kevin Johns and Swansea Sound, Adrian Davies and the Vale of Glamorgan Hotel, The Marriott Hotel Swansea, Ian Williams (Combined Life), Diff'rent Records of London & Wales, Richard Lillicrap for his accounting and Wayne Davies of Amman Sports Tours.

All photographs are reproduced with the expressed permission of the owners, *The Western Mail, Daily Star*, *South Wales Evening Post*, *South Wales Argus*, Allsport, Rivals.net, Phil Sumbler, Gary Martin at www.scfc.co.uk, and Roger Freestone.

Keith Haynes has been writing on the subject of Welsh football for a number of years. He started out as a fanzine contributor in the late 1980s and has since written for *Total Football* magazine, the national press and various football related papers. He still writes for the unofficial Swansea City magazine, *Jackplug*, and has diversified into more mainstream writing. Originally from West Wales, Keith now lives and works in Gloucester.

Phil Sumbler runs the RogerFreestone.com website, Glamorgan Rivals website, JackArmy.net, and was co-author with Keith on the Tempus football title *Vetch Field Voices*. He is a lifelong Swansea City fan and a native of the city itself.

You can contact them at – Keith: Ry Media PO Box 19, Gloucester, GL3 4YA; Phil: PO Box 526, Clydach, Swansea, West Glamorgan.

INTRODUCTION

Work on *Another Day at the Office* began in earnest in the summer of 2000 as Keith and Phil completed their first book together, *Vetch Field Voices*. Not pretending to be great authors, the book is seen as a testament to a career of loyalty. The problems encountered when writing about someone's life are there for all to see. Memory will always fail at times, and hours and hours of research only means you may 'just' get it right.

You are not about to read about a glamorous superstar earning thousands each week who hides away in the glossy pages of *Hello* magazine. That is not Roger's way, and even if it had been on offer it would have been turned down. This is a basic story of a simple and dedicated life – the fact that he plays football and is adored by many fans means nothing. At the end of it all, when you meet Roger Freestone, you realise that he does not play at being a superstar and that there is no need to be in awe of a man who does his own gardening!

It is not always easy to get all the facts, and the authors have spent many days away from the luxuries of home to try and get this story to be as accurate as they can. Roger's propensity for madness does not help either. His mind is years ahead of its time – which means that his memory is going, not helpful at three o' clock in the morning when you are looking for that crucial South East Counties result against Millwall. But it has been an interesting journey, and a long one. Sadly, there are people out there only too willing to remain unhelpful – and of course they have that right. But the huge army of people who assisted in the gathering of information have been the making of this book.

Not every detail that the reader would like to be included will be here, but the main memories are well documented. This is not the story of a man who has travelled far and wide, but it is the story of a man who has repaid Welsh football the faith that it has shown in him. Away from the pitch he has asked that several people be included, and of course the text may not always be favourable – but nobody's life is all honey and light. This is the first back to basics football biography for a long time and we would like to think that, like the first few rounds of the FA Cup, it is interesting, and throws up a few surprises. This is grass roots stuff with no thrills, no transfer bungs or illegal payouts behind closed doors – in fact football as it should maybe always be seen, through the life of an honest and dedicated professional player.

Family Life

Roger Freestone's family life was not based solely in Wales as many may assume. He is close to his parents, Eddie and Gloria, and the rest of his immediate family, and talks affectionately of childhood days spent with his grandfather and brother. Maybe this is the best place to start.

With his heritage, Roger could have been picked for England. Of course, being based in Gwent, with staunch Welsh parents, meant that he was always going to wear the red shirt (or green and yellow in this instance) of Wales instead of the three lions of England. He does, however, look back fondly to long holidays in Bedfordshire. Roger's paternal grandfather was English and born and bred in Bedford. For years he worked in the London Brickworks in the town, and spent his weekend nights at the firm's social club. Roger's grandmother, Doris Eileen, died when he was very young, and Roger did not get the opportunity to really get to know her. But Basil John Freestone is someone who Roger remembers affectionately, recalling that – 'He was a loveable rogue, and definitely had the youngster still in him even in his later years. I loved going to Bedford with John and spending long holidays with him. We used to hang about the streets up there in Stewartby for hours and hours, and when the weather was good we would go to the open air swimming pool. It was an extremely good time to be a child. I know everyone harps on about it, but back then it was easy to do. There wasn't the problems we have today, like drugs in the forefront of our society, so it was never a worry for our parents. We had loads of friends up there too, and it got to a stage where I considered the lads in Stewartby as mates as much as the tight-knit gang we had in Rogerstone.'

Roger and John would run amuck in the town, while his parents and Basil listened to the acts and turns in the club and talked away the evenings. Basil was on his own at this time and enjoyed the family visits. Roger had an affinity with the social club's fruit machines, and enjoyed watching the men putting a week's wages in to the machines in the hope that they would hit the jackpot. When they did of course the money went straight back in. Nothing changes.

Basil John Freestone was from Stewartby and worked the ships for many years prior to the Second World War. A proud Royal Navy seaman, he worked as a stoker on destroyer ships serving all over the world. Eddie is proud to talk of Basil as a hard man, but someone you could look up to. Earning medals for his involvement in the Russian convoys of 1943 he had a touch of the 'Uncle Alberts' when his ship was sunk in the Mediterranean just before the war ended. From there he went on to work at the brick makers. Basil met Roger's grandmother, Doris, in Newport and when married she moved to Bedfordshire to set up home with him. Judith, Roger's sister, would also visit her grandfather, and all three children were devastated when Basil died in 1980. Doris had died six years earlier in 1974 and Roger recalls that – 'It hit my old man pretty hard I have to say, he was a different person for some time after that. We didn't go to the funeral; we were probably a bit too young, and in a way I was glad – I wouldn't have liked to have been there for that. But he was a good man, and as I said a likeable old rogue, always playing you up, I suppose the sort of grandfather we all had or wanted.'

On Roger's mother's side of the family, William and Joyce, Gloria's parents, are still alive today and, in Roger's words, 'both about a hundred and four or thereabouts'. Based in Abertillery, his mother's home town, they had thirteen children – Gloria being one of seven sisters. Eddie met Gloria at Llanwern steelworks in 1961. 'They didn't have any tele back then' Eddie jokes, 'but it was different then, work was plentiful, if you wanted it that is. I remember I took Gloria out for the first time in 1962, I suppose it was inevitable we would get married and we were very happy together.'

The couple settled in the Gwent area, and Roger was born in August 1968. Relatives away from the immediate family is not a major priority for Roger, his uncle in Australia being one of the few who he can honestly say is was closer member than most. Paul, who settled in Perth, Australia when Roger was a small child seeks out his nephew every time he returns back home to Wales. Now a successful businessman in Perth, with three children, the homeland is a long way from home, but Roger looks forward to the day he can take his family out to see his uncle.

On Roger's wife's side are her parents, Ivor and Sheila, and Sue's brother, Steve, fondly known as Stavros, who remains a close friend of Roger – 'Well, he can be a pain in the arse can Stavros, but he is a good friend to me too. We have had a few run ins with each other; he has the knack of winding me up a bit at times. On my stag night I lost it a bit with him, and put him through Sheila and Ivor's new plateglass door. It was just drunken madness, and looking back now it's funny, but at the time Ivor was bloody livid. Like all good family run ins they shouldn't last forever.' Stavros lives alone in a flat in Risca with his dog and, like his brother Martin, who works at Burtons Biscuits in Gwent, still keep Roger on his toes now and again. 'The pair of them are a good laugh, and like to wind it in to me as often as they can, but over the years I have come to accept the fact they are nutters, and also good friends.'

Close friends to Roger and Susan are at a premium, and that clearly is the way that Roger likes to keep it. As a professional footballer he likes to get home and be with the family, and when at home he keeps himself very much to a close network of friends. 'I do know a lot of people, but very few of them I would call my friends – those who are close to us, well, I do enjoy their company, and it's a great release from the pressures of football.'

Colin and Lisa Bushell (Colin having been given the nickname of 'Stanley' by Roger) are the sort of people he likes to mix with when the pressure is right off. 'They are good friends, and they live close by to us, we enjoy getting away for a few days, even if it's down to West Wales with the kids; they are good company, and keep my feet on the ground. We have other close friends in Risca, Vikki and Neil Griffiths, they used to live by us before we moved, and Dave and Natalie Crandon, who Sue and I have got to know very well through their son Ryan who has excema, but apart from that I am a private person, and that's the way I like it.'

At home, both Dan and Lauren take up the majority of Roger's time away from his hobby of DIY. Dan now plays for the Cardiff City youth development side – they are, of course, his closest team to home – and Roger still trains a local side, Gelli under-11s, with his friend, Chris Dudden.

Sue's sister, Deborah, is married to Dean and both live nearby in High Cross. Roger was proud to be asked to be godfather to their daughter, Lynsey, as was Sue to be asked to be godmother.

All in all, one gets the feeling that Roger likes the quiet life and nothing too stressful away from the Saturday roar and sundry pressures of football. Although Roger's life could be a lot busier and more manic with booze, clubs and parties (even in Gwent!), he has chosen to keep it simple and relaxed. Roger now has his career firmly established in his mind, but getting there was some journey, that was not easy and never stable. He made it, however, and the people and events referred to in this book have all played their part in the Roger Freestone story.

Roger Freestone with his sister, Judith.

The Freestone family with Roger's grandfather, Basil. Roger is in the Welsh colours.

Roger on holiday with John and Judith.

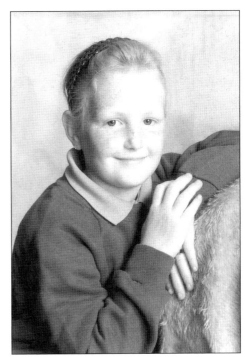

Roger's two children, Dan and Lauren.

Roger and Sue on holiday.

Left: Lauren, wearing her dad's team strip. Right: Roger Freestone and Ryan Giggs pose with Dan.

Roger and Dan, wearing his Tottenham shirt.

Sue on holiday.

Sue and Roger on their wedding day.

After the marriage ceremony in Wales.

Dan and Lauren in their Welsh rugby tops.

The Goalkeeper

Roger Freestone is a goalie. Since he can remember he has been involved in football, from his early days as a midfielder for Cefnwood school, Rogerstone in Gwent to taking the world stage as a Welsh international custodian at The Millennium Stadium there has only been one aim: to be the best at what he does.

Roger is no journeyman footballer struggling from club to club, with tales of a season here and a season there to talk of. He is different. Since 1991 he has held the position of Swansea City's number one choice between the sticks. Over these ten years, Roger has broken many records as a Swansea player. Before that he was a Chelsea regular and Championship medal winning player after signing from Newport County, a club which he still holds close to his heart. He could have easily moved on – rumours of where have always been a subject of great interest for Welsh football fans.

This book tells you about the significant performances and the clubs. It also covers his football relationships, which reads like a who's who of managers, players and coaches. To the few who have got close to Roger Freestone, in itself a very hard thing to do, he is a good friend and a down-to-earth person, a quality many would like to think they have, but few possess. Those that have known him all his life speak proudly of their funny and sad memories with the man.

Some people will read these pages and struggle to comprehend his life and football career that should have led him by now to be a Premiership regular at the very least. But he has chosen a different path – a path of stability for his family and of not forgetting his roots and the reasons

why he still lives today in the same area that he was born and brought up. This is the underlying theme of Roger's story: keeping the basics simple, not letting anyone down and giving your all. He continues to travel from Newport to Swansea each day and train with a side that has offered so much in recent times, but delivered so little. It is a job, and hence the title of this book. For Roger, the day-to-day life of a football career is simply another day at the office.

1

TUMBLING DOWN AND GROWING UP
1968-1983

What better way could there be to start this book than Roger Freestone as a baby in free-fall? It took no time at all for the young Roger to make his mark on the green grass of Wales. At just eight months old with his mother Gloria and older brother John in a local park, he went tumbling down a steep slope. John was playing on the swings, his mother keeping him happy by pushing him back and forward, John's screams of joy holding her concentration. Parked close by was Roger in his buggy. Was it the excited screams of his brother that made Roger move and trip the buggy's brake? Maybe so, but his frantic movements took him on a journey that just could have seen the end of the future international footballer before it all started. For whatever reason the buggy slipped towards a drop that an adult would pause at before negotiating. And Roger was gone.

His mother recounts the moment: 'We were in High Cross Park; John is a few years older than Roger so I was pushing him on the swings, Roger was in his new pushchair. One second he was there, the next he was gone. It takes a while to take in a situation like that, I couldn't comprehend what was going on. I ran to the edge of the swing park and looked down. Roger was there upside down in his pushchair – he was okay thankfully, nothing permanent, well, nothing on the surface,' Gloria laughs, 'He was a football mad boy, always kicking a ball, it was like it was attached to his feet. He would run around the back garden for hours and hours, he caused more damage to our back garden than a herd of cattle. Maybe that fall he had has a lot to do with what he does today, being a footballer.' Edward Freestone, Roger's father, takes up the tale, 'Roger was forever outside, in the end I built a new fence line, like a training area for him to play in, you couldn't stop him. From the age of two he would always have a football with him, no matter where we went. We lived in Tudor Crescent in High Cross at the time. The neighbours must have thought he was mad. But isn't that how all footballers start? Just kicking a ball about and learning all the skills? That was Roger. I never dreamed he would go on to do what he has done, but when you think about it, he had the talent from an early age. He was always being asked to play football, no matter where or with who. He would play three times a weekend as a boy, for the school, Newport Schools, Risca Rangers, Lliswerry Stars – he was always playing football.

The thing with Roger was that he was always ten years older in his head, which maybe for a footballer is a very good thing indeed. He had his mind set and that was it, there was no telling him. As soon as he went out at the end of school, it was to play football. John, his brother, also loved football, but even he got fed up from time to time; Roger just never got bored with it.'

Roger's talents were identified at an early age, but not as a goalkeeper. At Cefnwood school he played in midfield. Keith James, then a teacher at the school but now retired, spotted Roger's talent. As manager of the junior second eleven and working with Bob Sully in charge of the first team, Roger found himself selected as an outfield player in his early days. Roger loved his days at Cefnwood, where the lack of pressure on the sports field produced a philosophy he has never forgotten – that of enjoying the day. Initially he played, in his own words, as a 'midfield general'. His heroes of the time were Cruyff and Beckenbauer; like every young child of the time, Roger found himself copying the skills of these players, such as Cruyff turns and twenty-five-yard banana shots. By his own admission his studies would never get him noticed. He struggled academically, but found solace on the football field, his talents compensating for his classroom torment when it came to mathematics and English.

Cefnwood were a good school side, and Roger was pivotal to the team. So much so, in fact, that if they were playing a poor side he would play out, and if the opposition were better he would play in goal. A certain Mr Everson, the school's headmaster, kept the young Freestone in check without realising it. He operated a strict environment, and when Roger found himself in the man's presence he admits to being terrified. On one occasion, Roger was sent from the classroom for getting his vowels wrong. 'What are you doing here boy?' boomed Mr Everson. Petrified, Roger stuttered a reply he saw as self preservation, blurting out that another boy had just run out of the school and had been fighting. As the intimidating figure of Mr Everson whirled away to find the young hoodlum, Roger breathed a sigh of relief. He was terrified of him as a teacher, and his awe of such an authority figure kept him in check.

Today, the wheel has turned and Roger is looked up to by many young football fans, but back in the mid-1970s at Cefnwood, Mr Everson ruled with an iron fist and Roger spent much of his time keeping out of his way. 'I just told him a boy had just run away from the school, he shot off looking for him, but my word was he a strict man. He used to fill me with fear, everyone remembers a man like that at school and every school must have had a Mr Everson. I think that if I saw him now I would still be fearful of him and call him "Sir" as much as he wanted me to.'

Roger's time at Cefnwood was successful, the team reaching a number of school cup finals. In turn this enabled him to play for the Gwent under-11 team, an honour for someone so young. In one final, Roger discovered how cruel the game of football could be. Cefnwood were drawing 0-0 and the game went into extra time. Because of the importance of the tie, Roger was in goal. Throughout the game he had very little to do but was frustrated to see his team miss a number of gilt-edged chances. With minutes to go, a mis-hit shot screwed off the turf and Roger felt he had the chance well covered. Cue the god of football inevitability – the shot went straight through his legs, taking a course that he just could not have envisaged. For days after the final he blamed himself for the loss, and ran the scenario through his mind on so many occasions it made him feel ill. As time went on he began to realise that the perils of life itself were far more important, but as a youngster in a crucial cup game nothing else mattered. It might as well have been Wembley as Gwent; maybe this was a prophetic moment?

Roger's stable upbringing is not lost on him. His brother, John, and sister, Judith, were lucky to have in their parents a solid foundation that reflects Roger's appreciation of what many people consider very basic values, although there was the occasional youthful misdemeanor. 'We were a normal family to an extent, nothing unusual, all three children were well looked after, our dad worked hard, as did my mother. There was little to worry me as a child. Dad worked at Llanwern steelworks, fact is he has worked there most of his life, and Mum always had the odd job to keep the money coming in. I was lucky, it was a time when you could roam about and play all day in the holidays. We used to get in to the usual trouble. There was a sweet factory down the road from us in Rogerstone, Moffat's it was called, we used to play football there a lot using the delivery shutters as goals. Of course when the factory used to close at night the temptation after a kick-about was too much, and we used to help ourselves to sweets in the factory. The shutters were never properly closed and all of us had as many sweets as we wanted for months. The same thing used to happen at the bread factory, we used to run off to the woods and stuff our faces with bread! You wouldn't eat the stuff at home, but this was different. But of course the police soon put us off, they knew what was going on, and a few visits from the police to my old man sorted me out. Another good place to play football was at The Welfare playing fields; one day a friend of mine, Steve Thomas, had some matches and we set the field on fire, just messing about, no damage as such, and the grass needed cutting anyway. On our way home Steve had a pocket full of matches, and someone stopped us and told us the field had been set on fire. I remember saying, "You can search us if you like, it wasn't us." Fire engines screamed about, and that sort of told me that a life of crime was not for me. It was just youthful stupidity, and to be honest if you haven't done stuff like that as a kid you haven't lived or are telling lies.'

The rural aspect of the area appealed to Roger – days spent hanging around with friends in fields in the summer, playing football, fishing and generally doing nothing are the days we all should remember as a child. Rogerstone can be found at the foot of a hill that leads from the M4 motorway, a convenient place as any to commute from and a few miles from Risca. It's as tranquil as anywhere can be these days, with the lure of the big city a few miles away, and the industrial town of Newport employing many of the area's population. New houses have been set up for the local community to buy, another part of the reason why the Freestone family have never ventured too far away. Eddie Freestone explains, 'The area is friendly as far as I am concerned, they will carry me away in a box the day I leave, there's no need for me or Gloria to move. I am retired now from the steelworks, and there couldn't have been a better time to go with all the redundancy about. John [Roger's brother] has just been made redundant from the steelworks, it's not a good time. But Roger had a good time here, we are in a way a protective community on the edge of bigger things, we know what is what and people from outside may not like it here. But that's our life, and Roger seems to like it, he could have moved anywhere to play football, and initially he did, but I knew he would always settle here. It's worked out well for him.' Some may think of a 'local shop for local people', but, as Eddie says, 'It's the way – you have a choice if you don't like it, and the M4 can easily take you elsewhere.'

If Cefnwood introduced a young Roger Freestone to football, then Bassaleg school, a rugby-dominated comprehensive, would turn out the finished article. At the age of eleven Roger started at the school, and was immediately thrown into rugby union. Initially he was to play at inside half, eventually taking up a position of full back. Eddie remembers it well, 'This was a time when Roger was good at all sports, and rugby was no different; he was a very fast and effective full back, playing one season at the school. He was filling out a bit and no longer a slight boy but developing into a big teenager. I wouldn't have minded at all if he went on to play rugby, but deep down we knew that football was his real game. He was playing local club football for Lliswerry; now there was a team that won everything.'

Eddie is quite correct, Lliswerry are documented as winning everything from 1977 to 1983, and tough competition from Newport YMCA and Cromwell enhanced the standard. Parents would do battle on the touch lines, sometimes quite literally when the occasion overcame the usual normal thinking of the adult watchers. These were big local teams with county players and displayed the very best Gwent had to offer on a football field. The pressure of these big games reflected in the performances of the children playing. Too scared to lose, they would give frequent glances towards their parents across the field of play for guidance only to see arguments and, at times, physical contact. This did none of them any good at all. The local press of the day refers to tough standards and commitment beyond that expected of such young people, Lliswerry's main opponents being Newport YMCA. Roger would stay with the club until he signed for Newport County and he quickly learned that these games were the local derbies that provoked real passion. A young man by the name of Paul Coldrick would also follow Roger to County, but other budding talents like Heath Twist disappeared into oblivion, much to Roger's amazement. Twist was a class product of the local schools and county sides. He went one way and Roger the other, which shows just how lucky the future professionals of the day were to find their signatures on contracts.

Mixing your football teams at the highest of youth levels was not a worry at all. No matter the challenge – be it Lliswerry, Risca, Newport schools or playing in full internationals for Wales – it was always just another game for Roger. Whilst at Lliswerri, Roger also played for another top local side, Risca Rangers. Again, Risca were very dominant in their area and Roger found himself with players like Simon Harrison. On Saturdays he would be the main reason that Risca remained on top of youth football at the time, while on Sundays he reverted to playing with Lliswerry.

At thirteen, Roger was beginning to be noticed on a bigger stage. Having been selected for Newport Schools, he was to become an automatic choice. Adrian Jones, then secretary of the Newport and District Schools FA, was watching Roger closely and would eventually secure his signature for Newport County. Being in the shop window of Wales scouts was also to prove fruitful – although little did he know that he was being earmarked as an international goalkeeper at beginning of his teenage years. Newport Schools set the local classrooms alight with their performances in 1983. Reaching the final of the BHS shield in the April of that year they played Mid-Cheshire schools. A two-legged game saw both sides still level at 0-0, with the decision to award the shield to both sides probably being the right one. Roger played in both games and it was noticed that without his incredible athleticism the result would have been very different. The very next season, in the same competition, Roger would face Des Trick, Chris Coleman and Dean Saunders as Newport Schools took on Swansea Schools (then twenty-eight time winners of the Welsh version of the tournament). Newport would despatch their opponents over two legs 2-1.

Roger's games for Newport Schools and the Gwent county side were impressive, and at the age of fourteen Roger earned an international squad call-up for the under-15 squad. Travelling to Tynecastle, in Edinburgh as the replacement goalkeeper was fine. When he was told he had been selected his head was spinning, although he knew that his involvement would be minimal, as he was still playing with players older than himself. His father agrees, 'Roger was always playing one or even two years above his standard, even for the local sides he was playing with boys two years older than he was'. John Freestone remembers playing for Risca Rangers at the same time as Roger. 'I was fifteen and Roger was twelve, nearly thirteen; he was playing a good two years above his age for the season we actually played together. Thinking back that was a great time for me, Roger was well known locally as a class goalie for his age, and I was able to play with him when we won the league championship. I'm not sure if Roger took it all in, just what he was capable of achieving really, he seemed to take it all in his stride, and it's that quality that makes him a winner. He had more cups and trophies than our local jewellers, and I remember we had a look at them all one day. He had a great big box of trophies from winners medals to player of the season trophies, and only one runners-up medal. That box was massive, he could hardly carry it down the stairs. I remember Roger looked at the runners-up medal and said "Bad season that John". I laughed – a bad season! Winning a medal for the best side in town, what can you say?'

Roger wasn't to wait too long before earning his first cap, playing for Wales under-15s against Scotland at Abertillery Park. The game was drawn 3-3, although Roger's memory of it is not good. He just recalls enjoying the day, and although in his usual tizz at the expectation of a match he was surprised to find that he wasn't too nervous. He went to play some thirteen games at that level thereafter. In Dublin he inspired the national side to a 2-0 victory over the Republic and earned many plaudits. Roger was now playing football five days and evenings a week. Local press spoke freely about the young man with a great future in the professional game. So much so that local football league side Newport County were to line him up for a schoolboy contract, although they were nearly beaten to his signature by, of all teams, Manchester United. United had a massive chain of scouts and sleeping coaches in the South Wales area, and Roger's talent was not going unnoticed. After all, how could they not notice a player who was an international with players two years older than himself, and who was regularly selected for Newport Schools and the county side?

Eddie is reluctant to talk at length about Roger's chances away from Newport at this time, but admits that his son could have gone anywhere. 'I will tell you this much now, the scouts in South Wales were very aware of Roger's quality as a goalkeeper. Read the papers of the day, loads of contact was made regards Roger. You would see him playing for Newport Schools and there would be a whole load of scouts there – it was like a who's who of football clubs. He played up at Reading for the schools side and I counted twenty-three scouts from any club you wish to mention in the top flight. And Roger played a blinder, the wind was swirling all around the place and he was magnificent. From then on in he could have gone anywhere. I know for a fact that Leeds United wanted him, that's for sure, and Manchester United wanted him up there for six weeks. Then there was both of the Bristol clubs – City, now they've wanted him for years, that's always been a rumour, and one I can confirm. And Cardiff City were never far away. But of course he was contracted to Newport, and they had an eye for a large fee for him.'

Roger had indeed caught the eye of many scouts from all over the country. Roger left much of the contact with the big clubs to his father. Roger was still, in the eyes of his parents and the law, a child. Deep down, however, he was aware of the interest, and spent many nights thinking about the possibility of being a professional footballer. It was almost inevitable that this would be the path he would tread, it was just a matter of where that would be, and who would earn the signature of Wales' brightest young goalkeeper.

Roger in an early school photograph.

Roger with his brother, John.

Roger (back row, third on the right) in the outfield strip of Cefnwood Juniors.

Roger wears the goalkeeper's jersey at Cefnwood Juniors.

Lliswerry All Stars under-10s proudly display their honours.

Lliswerry All Stars under-16s.

Roger (back row, far right) lines up for the Newport under-13s side.

Roger's school photograph from Bassaleg Comprehensive in 1983.

2
NEWPORT OF CALL
1983-1987

As Roger started on his impressive run of form at youth level, it came as no real surprise when scouts from Newport County took note of his career. Newport is often viewed as the third ranked town/city in South Wales, and the football club certainly was the poor relation of both Swansea and Cardiff at the time, but you couldn't take away their European adventures, which gripped the whole of the country in the 1980s.

The town had not seen much development in the 1970s, being sandwiched almost halfway between Cardiff and Bristol. It did, however, have the major advantage of just being down the road from Roger's home in Rogerstone, and was an easy bus ride for a schoolboy to take if necessary. Being a local boy, it was no surprise when, in 1981, Roger signed schoolboy forms for Newport. For a budding professional footballer, this was a major thrill as Welsh football was experiencing a revival through the on-pitch antics of both Newport and Swansea City. Colin Addison was the man who signed Roger on schoolboy terms for the club – just twelve months after guiding Newport County to the quarter-finals of the European Cup Winners Cup, drawing a massive crowd into the tiny Somerton Park ground to see them exit the competition over two legs. On paper at least, Newport were not a big club, but that European run had certainly attracted the attention of the locals and Roger was no exception.

Roger continued to play football for his local sides whilst a schoolboy with Newport County, and his game continued to develop. At this time, Newport County themselves began to decline as the European exploits become more and more of a distant memory. The club were beginning to slip down the ladders of the Football League, but this was not something that was about to extinguish the flame of the young Roger's dream.

After two years of schoolboy football at Newport, the club decided that they had a potential star in the making and offered Roger apprentice terms in 1983 at the age of fifteen. Most schoolboys dream of signing terms for their first club in front of a large crowd on a Saturday afternoon, with the crowd all showing their appreciation. This was also to prove just a dream for Roger, as one evening before a reserve team game at Somerton Park, he and his father Eddie were present in the secretary's office at the ground to sign his first contract. The figure on that contract for the local boy finally entering the big world of professional football was £25 per week.

Professional football is a world that is often viewed from the outside as a glamorous place where fame is instant, and you are watched by thousands of people who would give anything to swap places with you. Roger was fully aware that there was a lot of hard work to be done before this particular world became a reality to him, and he was to realise some truths about apprentice football when he reported for duty on his very first day.

Roger had signed apprentice forms at the same time as another young boy that Newport had great hopes for, and, as they both came in on that first day, Roger was presented with someone around the same age as himself, with long hair and a Bristolian accent (the ideal image for a footballer at the time, although maybe without the West Country burr). As he shook hands with a young Darren Peacock, they both knew that there would be many highs and lows on the road to stardom.

The assumption of an apprentice footballer tends to be that you have to do such things as sweep the terraces of the ground and clean the boots of those above you that had already made the grade. Neither Roger or Darren expected to be faced with the challenge that they had that first day back in 1985, however. 'Welcome to Somerton Park and Newport County AFC' was the greeting from Dave Williams as he handed the two apprentices a Flymo lawnmower for them to cut the grass on the pitch and make it suitable to play football on! This was the harsh reality for two young men setting out on their chosen career. The pair spent most of the day with the Flymo, walking up and down the football pitch, wondering exactly what they had let themselves in for. As they carried out such duties, the shared experience created a friendship that was to last to this day, despite the two players heading their separate ways.

Roger grew used to a rigid routine as he went through his apprentice career and knew that if he was to make the full grade he would need to stick to his morning routine under strict observation from Dave Williams, the coach for the younger players.

Like most teenagers, Roger was very partial to a bit of sleep in the mornings and devised for himself a timetable to ensure that he was in the ground for the required 9 a.m. start. The alarm would wake Roger at 8.10 and he was out of bed in a flash to wash and get changed ready for the day. The bus from Rogerstone into Newport was 8.20 on the dot and, with a few close shaves, Roger would be at the bus stop just as the bus arrived for the twenty-minute trip into Newport town centre. From there he would have to wait another five minutes for the bus to Somerton Park, which would get him there at dead on 9.00 to face the sight of (without fail) Dave Williams waiting there with his watch.

After the exacting timekeeping routine, the strict regime continued as Roger, together with the other apprentices, had to put the kettle on and make the tea for the professionals when they started to arrive at the ground, usually around 9.30. As the pro's sat down to drink the results of the apprentice's hard work, it was on to the traditional boot cleaning. Apprentices were given a professional's boots to clean, and soon got used to the required standard – as well as the consequences of not meeting those requirements. Roger was tasked with cleaning the boots of

Linden Jones, a long-term professional of the club. Predictably, Linden's require-ment was that his boots were cleaned to such a standard that he could see his face in them.

Most of the time, using extra elbow grease, spit and polish, this was a task that Roger accomplished to a suitable standard not to provoke the wrath of Linden. He does remember, with a grin on his face, one occasion when the boots were not up to scratch . 'Linden had decided that the boots were not sufficient for his require-ments and that he could not glimpse his face in them. Linden obviously didn't feel that it would be enough punishment to just hand the boots back and ask me to clean them again.' Indeed, the retribution was to be far more severe as Linden and Mick Saxby took Roger into the bath before pulling down his shorts and under-pants. It was no surprise when the next instrument that Roger saw Linden holding was a disposable razor which was applied deftly to his genital region to remove half of his pubic hair. If that punishment wasn't bad enough, Roger remembers, with a degree of sadness, that 'My parents had also gone away for a week on holiday, but the punishment handed out by Linden was enough to mean that we could not indulge in what most teenagers would do with an empty house!'

Linden Jones has clear memories of Roger's time at the club. 'Like many appren-tices, Roger needed to be brought to book now and again. He was a bit of an upstart at times, and it was my way of keeping him in check. He had a big talent, that wasn't in doubt, and it wasn't as if he knew it, he just needed to be reminded what his position was at the club.' Linden also remembers a scar above his left eye that he believes was earned due to Roger's ineffectiveness in the penalty area under a one particular ball into the box. 'He just didn't come out for the cross and I got clattered by a big striker – but seriously, he was on a par with Andy Dibble at the time, he was very good indeed'. Linden Jones played for Newport, Reading and Cardiff City. He now works with Swansea's talented youth sides at The Vetch Field.

Paul Compton, Swansea's youth development officer, also remembers Roger well. 'I wasn't at the club for long when Roger was there, but being an ex-appren-tice that nearly never made it myself I had a lot in common with Roger. I was at Cardiff City when they "let me go" so to speak, and although Roger was good, you just never know what will happen in football. What I will say is that I was really surprised when Chelsea came in for him; he was very young, and I would say very gullible too – as much as we all are at that age. He was stitched up a bit with his wages, but he was happy enough, although he could have got more from what I heard at the time. He was a scruffy bugger, and at times was like Bambi on ice when he played, but he was a nice bloke too. He was one of the boys, and that helped him a lot, he would never be an outsider would Roger, never. Always having a laugh and always ripping the piss, that's Roger Freestone, and it has put him in good stead today. He now is the old sweat, and you can see that he is still a true and hard working pro. You can't say that he should have done better, he has done what we all would love to do. He plays professional football and represents his country. His international cap, if it's the only one he ever gets, reflects the dreams of millions of kids. He has played against the world's best and never let himself down. What else can you say? From Somerton Park to playing against Brazil, I would settle for that.'

Life as an apprentice often involved mischief and the occasional accident. Lottery tickets, even before the National Lottery days, were as much part of a professional football club then as they are now. Scratch cards were for sale on match days and throughout the week, with prizes as high as £1,000 on offer. These tickets were a vital source of income to all clubs in the lower reaches of the Football League, and Newport County was no exception to this. The lady in charge of the tickets at Newport during Roger's time with the club was called Anne. Anne had been a stalwart of Newport County for many years and was also Darren Peacock's landlady. She was like a mother to some of the younger players. Roger and some of his fellow apprentices decided that the wage of a potential pro was not enough to keep them in the manner to which they wanted to be accustomed. A plan was devised and the 'Fearsome Four' got their hands on a regular basis on a supply of these lottery tickets. The unsuspecting Anne paid out on these stolen tickets without question for weeks – after all, if you couldn't trust footballers at the club involved who could you trust?

Eventually the lottery ticket scam started to wear off. The odd small win here and there was not quite enough to send them into an early retirement from the game and they ceased to take more tickets. Anne, to this day, never knew what was happening.

Roger's ability to cost Newport money was becoming legendary amongst the apprentices and those in charge of them, as besides the lottery scam and collecting his wages each week, he also managed to destroy a ceiling of the main dining room at Somerton Park. Gary Burns, the head groundsman entrusted with the upkeep and maintenance of Somerton Park, took Roger into the VIP lounge one day and climbed a ladder, bought with him to gain access into the loft area of the lounge. It was winter time and there was a leak from the loft that was causing Gary some concern. Gary was always one for leading the mischief with the younger players and he asked Roger to follow him up into the loft. As with most things about Somerton Park at this time, the loft was not in the best condition. A wave of cold hit Roger as he entered and the musty smell was almost overpowering. As the young Freestone tried is best to demonstrate his agility and light-footedness, he lost his footing slightly and a size ten foot was placed through the ceiling into the main dining room. Luckily, Gary saw the funny side and the damage was repaired before questions could be asked as to who had caused it.

Despite such incidents, Roger was making an impression on the pitch and professional terms were just round the corner. On 2 April 1986, Jimmy Mullen, the then manager at the club, presented Roger with a contract for £80 per week, with additional payments on top. To an apprentice who had been earning just over a quarter of that, this was a small fortune and it was without hesitation that Roger put pen to paper and became a professional footballer. He knew as he signed his name at the bottom of that contract that he had to fight his way into the team as he wanted to earn the £25 appearance bonus plus £30 a win/£15 a draw on top of his basic wage.

The hard work put in over three years, as a schoolboy and then as an apprentice, had paid off, and the eighteen-year old Roger Freestone was finally a professional footballer. Newport County, however, were a side in rapid decline. League form on the pitch was poor and the side was facing relegation into the Fourth Division. Off the pitch, matters were just as bleak as County, along with many sides in the mid-1980s, were losing money as quickly as the team were losing matches. It was not the most glamorous time to be a professional footballer at Newport, let alone a first year professional but Roger was still determined to break into the first team and claim the number one jersey for himself.

Mark Kendall was the current first choice goalkeeper at the club and Roger initially had to be content with putting in some impressive performances for the reserves under John Macey. (Ironically, Roger also arrived at Swansea a few years later when Mark Kendall was first choice and again eventually managed to dislodge him.) Kendall was known to the other players at Newport as 'The Colonel' because 'it rhymes'. Mark was one of the best 'keepers playing in the lower divisions at this time and had previously played for more glamorous sides, including Spurs.

Despite the problems at Newport, these were fun times for the professionals. A good blend of experience in the likes of Terry Boyle and John Lewis was combined with the youth and enthusiasm of players like Roger and Darren Peacock, which created a great team atmosphere. Even training was popular. The Railway End at Somerton Park was the side of the ground at which the professionals competed in a six-a-side game every Friday towards the end of training. Maybe this was where Roger learned some of his silky ball playing skills, as these matches would invariably take place with no goalkeepers (and normally no rules either) – a great way to let off steam but not somewhere to learn your trade for a Saturday afternoon! Bobby Smith, the manager, used to watch on as his professionals, with six-inch stones marking the goalposts, played a match that was anything but friendly. The main object of these games seemed to be who could kick the most lumps out of someone else, something which often made Roger feel that playing in goal was possibly the best place to be.

In Christmas 1986, as the weather turned icy and most people contemplated cold turkey for a few weeks, Roger got the chance to make his professional debut for Newport County. As with most things at Newport, life was a struggle on the pitch at this point in time. Mark Kendall was not in the best form of his life and the team had just tasted another defeat on Boxing Day, when Roger was pulled to one side to be told he was playing in the next game. Panic set in as Roger realised that he was to finally play in the Football League in front of the biggest crowd of his life. Although not a great event in the overall scheme of things, to a young player it was a huge occasion that brought out the fear that maybe he wasn't as good as people told him he was.

By chance, Roger used to travel to and from matches with Mark at that time, and had to head home on Boxing Day with him, both of them aware that their roles were going to swap the next game. Mark decided to stop off for some liquid refreshment on the way home, and while he indulged in a beer or two, Roger sipped his orange juice thinking of his upcoming debut. In these days before mobile phones, Roger was also unable to contact Susan to tell her he was going to be later than planned. A nice family Boxing Day had been planned with her and her parents in a local club. When he eventually got home at 9 p.m., he told her the good news about his debut and headed off for an early night with all kinds of thoughts going through his head.

At the age of 18 years and 4 months, on 28 December 1986, Roger finally made his first-team debut for Newport and his first-ever League appearance as Port Vale travelled into Wales for a Third Division fixture. It was with a great deal of pride that Roger's father made the short trip into Newport that day to watch Roger in front of a sizeable holiday time crowd at Somerton Park. Joining Eddie at Somerton Park were Susan and her father, Ivor – maybe not quite the family outing that is traditional around the Christmas period, but one that they made willingly as the players took to the pitch and they witnessed that the man in the number one shirt for the home team was indeed their boy, Roger Freestone.

It was not a happy debut for Roger as the visitors, true to current form, ran out 2-0 winners. However, as the players grouped in the dressing room at the end of the game, Roger knew that the memories he carried off the pitch that day would stick with him for the rest of his life. A dream that had begun many years before when he first picked up a football was now full reality and he silently vowed to himself as he took off his goalkeeping jersey that this chance would be fully taken and it was now up to Mark Kendall to win the shirt back off him – he was in possession of the number one jersey, and that was how he intended it to stay!

As 1987 dawned, Roger maintained his position between the sticks at Somerton Park as the club slipped nearer the bottom of the table and further into financial trouble. The mood amongst the supporters was one of disbelief as they watched their team slipping into a relegation battle, and maybe into another battle that was to prove eventually to be far more serious.

Roger's appearance money continued to mount up as his run in the team continued, even if win bonuses were slightly thinner on the ground. Susan continued to be of great support in his early days in the team, driving to Newport to watch his games in their old green Cavalier. Life as a footballer was becoming routine and Roger was beginning to establish himself. Unbeknown to him, he was already attracting attentions from bigger clubs, who were monitoring his progress on a regular basis.

At this time, Middlesborough, one of the three clubs from the 'passionate' North East were in the doldrums and playing at their lowest level. For a local boy who had previously only played in front of a few thousand people, Ayresome Park was to prove to be a daunting experience and one not to forget; 14,000 people were present at the game that day and the atmosphere that hit Roger as he ran out onto the pitch with the rest of the team was one of the most intimidating experiences any eighteen-year-old professional could experience. Middlesborough were a team that belonged at a higher level and were hot favourites to pick up another three points against the struggling Welsh side. The crowd noise was deafening as the biggest game of Roger's fledgling career kicked off.

During the match, Roger was also to pick up another career first, as yet another Middlesborough attack saw one of their strikers started to advancing down for a one-on-one situation against him. There was no option for Roger, who advanced out of his area in a bid to win the ball. Unfortunately for him, on this occasion his timing was less than impeccable he clattered into the opponent as the ball ran loose and to safety. To a man, the Middlesborough fans bayed for the youngster's blood as the referee reached into his pocket for his notepad. They believed that there was no option but to dismiss him from the field of play.

Roger faced the referee and listened to the deafening noise all around him. His stomach lurched as he faced up to the fact that so near the start of his career he would be sent off and face a suspension. Fortunately it was not to be, as the referee only issued a caution and, as Roger ran back between the posts to face the free-kick, he heard the taunts and jeers of the home fans incensed that he was still on the pitch. Roger tried to place the incident to the back of his mind as the game continued. Deep-down, he knew that maybe he should have been sent off, which would have had disastrous consequences on his budding career. Ten years on and he certainly would have been – but this was the 1980s and referees were just a little more lenient at the time. The lack of a dismissal was crucial to Roger's progress, as his run continued in the team through the rest of the winter and into spring.

As most of Wales celebrated St David's Day, speculation was rife around the Newport ground that a bid for Roger from Tottenham was imminent. Roger and Susan had many times discussed this possibility – it was a move that they were not sure that they wanted to take, but maybe a necessity rather than an option to the young couple. Another player had been loaned to Newport from Tottenham because he needed first-team football. Tim O'Shea's arrival seemed to indicate that Spurs would be on the look out for a replacement at White Hart Lane, and a swap deal seemed the logical answer for both clubs.

The club was in serious trouble off the pitch, with money worries mounting almost daily. The fees that would be involved in Roger's transfer would help the club, and this was something that played on his mind as he mulled over the possibility. To an eighteen-year-old who had lived in a small village in Wales all his life, London was a massive place and very daunting – particularly as he had less than a year's first-team professional experience.

On 9 March 1986, Newport faced a Sunday fixture against Chesterfield at Somerton Park. It was a typical Third Division fixture with three points being essential as the side looked to try and stay in the division. Roger put all the transfer speculation to the back of his mind as he took his place in the game. Chesterfield were a reasonable side, and it was with great relief all round that Newport ran out 1-0 winners in the game, gaining valuable points and adding a win bonus to that week's pay packet for the players. As the team celebrated the victory in the dressing room after the match, a message came to Roger that he was to report to the boardroom as soon as possible once he had changed. Although he guessed that this was regarding the projected move to Spurs, he was still scared as he waited outside the boardroom door.

As he walked into the room, he was greeted with the sight of Archie Menzies, Newport's chairman at the time, Richard Ford, another director, and the joint management team of John Lewis and Dave Williams. Roger sat down at the table with them and was told that Chelsea, rather than Tottenham, had tabled a bid of £160,000. This was to be paid as £95,000 up front, with the further payments relating to the number of appearances he was to make for the club. This was money that Newport County were in no position to refuse and, in reality, the deal was all but signed and sealed. Roger had many thoughts running through his mind as he left the ground to meet Susan, who used to wait for him in the car over the railway bridge.

That particular day, however, because he had been so long, she had presumed that he had already made his own way home and had left without him. Roger sat down that evening to discuss the move with his father, believing that Eddie would make the right decision in this kind of situation. Roger's father is a shrewd man and warned his son of the pitfalls of discussing terms with a big club, telling him to be 'cute' when discussing the terms of his new contract.

One of Roger's greatest regrets is not asking his dad to attend Stamford Bridge with him. Eddie had insisted on attending, but Roger wanted to prove that he could do everything for himself – he was, after all, going to be a footballer with a big club. Roger was given one final piece of advice as far as his contract went, his father telling him to remember that he was in the driving seat when discussing terms, as Chelsea wanted him.

Roger spent a sleepless few hours the night before travelling up to London. He was struggling to believe that this move was happening. He was leaving home and all his family to start a new life. His father neatly summed it up for him, 'Look Son, Newport are in the shit with money, God knows if there will be a football club next year. This move is for the best. And they need the money, God do they need the money.' That blunt statement made Roger realise that he had to go. He loved County but was clever enough to realise that they needed him to make this move more than he needed the home comforts of life in Gwent. As he eventually drifted off to sleep, he dreamt of playing for Chelsea at Old Trafford. The following morning, Roger arrived at Somerton park at 7 a.m. to travel to Stamford Bridge with John Lewis and Dave Williams, to meet the Chelsea manager, John Hollins.

The trio arrived in West London at 11 a.m. and Roger was very quickly offered a contract of £150 per week. By 2 p.m. that afternoon he was officially a Chelsea player, having posed for the traditional signing-on photo call with John Hollins and club secretary Shelia Marston. Hollins touted Roger as a great signing, and made a statement that was prophetic 'This man can carry on playing until he is forty, if he keeps himself fit and does the right things in life'. John Hollins may have made many mistakes according to some fans of QPR, Chelsea and Swansea – but this time he certainly got it right.

Less than twenty-four hours earlier, Roger had lined up in a Newport County jersey for a vital League match to avoid the drop into the basement division. Now, he was 150 miles from home and a First Division footballer. It was, to coin a phrase, worlds apart from where he had grown up and what he knew, but this was almost an inevitable move for a goalkeeper with his talent. Roger had never been to a stadium as big as Stamford Bridge before, the only comparison he could make was Ayresome Park. John Hollins took Roger out for lunch on the Kings Road to celebrate the transfer, before the newest Chelsea player set off for Newport to pass on the news to his family.

Like Newport, Chelsea were fighting a relegation battle, the only difference being that they were several divisions higher and boasted a far greater pedigree than his previous club. Eddie Niedzwiecki was the incumbent Chelsea goalkeeper who Roger would have to displace. This was a player that Roger now freely admits he had never heard of before signing for the Blues – in fact, he had no idea where Chelsea were in the League until he signed his first contract at Stamford Bridge, such was his devotion to his homeland.

Part of the deal that took Roger to Chelsea allowed him to play on loan at Somerton Park until the end of the season, although things did not work out that way. Unfortunately for Roger, he was called back to London to spend the remainder of the season with Chelsea. His return to London was a disaster for Newport. Although the club had suffered some heavy defeats, Roger could not be blamed as the club were approaching their terminal demise – which ultimately led to bankruptcy and loss of League status. Roger had returned to London to be a Chelsea player, but every Wednesday (Chelsea's day off) he would be back at Somerton Park to be with the rest of the Newport team, such was his love of the club.

At the end of that season, however, the time had come to cut all ties with Newport and become a fully fledged Chelsea player. The local hero was entering the big time.

Roger steps out for pre-season training with Newport County.

Roger and Darren Peacock on their very first day with Newport County.

The Newport County squad, 1985. Roger is in the second row from the back. Linden Jones is in the same row, third from the left.

Roger with team-mates, including Leighton James (front row, centre) and Mark Kendall (back row, fourth right).

3

THE CHELSEA YEARS
1987-1991

Roger's signing for Chelsea is still is the biggest move he has had to make. He was leaving home, his family unit was to be left behind and it was the end of his childhood as such. Although he was excited the evening before he joined Chelsea, he was also close to tears – he was making the move that the majority of people make at some time, but was very close to his father and consequently under a lot of pressure.

The confusion and culture shock of the move and settling in at Chelsea is best described by Roger himself, 'That night me and dad had a long conversation. It seemed to me that he was very happy about the move, he maybe even had a hunch about it; he's clever like that. He told me to be very cute when discussing terms, and to be honest he should have come with me but he had work to go to at the steelworks. At one point he insisted on coming, but I wanted to do it for myself. He told me what to ask for, and insisted that it was Chelsea who wanted me and I was in the driving seat. I should have listened to him. That night I didn't sleep much, I was finding hard to take it all in. I looked around my bedroom, it was all very final really. I just knew I wanted to go, but I didn't if you know what I mean. I was at Newport, living at home and very happy with Susan. Why would I want to leave? … The next morning was a blur, one minute we were in Newport, the next in one of the big Chelsea offices. I suddenly felt very alone. John Lewis was there, but he was not alongside me, I felt distant and helpless. I was no longer a Newport player, I was a Chelsea player. John moved away from the table, I was there with John Hollins and some other people who I did not know. I just signed the forms. John Hollins was the current manager, and he was having a hard time from the fans, something in later years he would have at Swansea. He seemed nice enough but very distant. He was edgy and so was I. They took me to the training ground where I met Peter Bonetti, the goalkeeping coach – it was all very hard to take in. Whilst I stood there at the training ground I said to Peter, "Where are we in the league." It was then I realised that I knew nothing at all about anything outside of Newport. I was to do some growing up in the next few months, that was for sure. Then I said, "Where do I live" Peter smiled, I must have sounded stupid or something, he had seen it all before, and I have seen it many times since. I was lost, lonely and on £150 a week, it should have been more but I didn't care. At that point I could have cried and gone home. I looked at my contract, it was for a basic fee which would rise to £300 in time. Then I saw a clause at the bottom. I couldn't believe it, I had ten grand in the bank as a signing on fee. That cheered me up no end.'

'Also at the club was Eddie Niedzwiecki, a quality goalkeeper in my opinion, and Tony Godden was there too. I was surrounded with quality, although what I soon realised was that even though these players were very good, Chelsea were struggling. Ken Bates was there and pulling all the strings. John Hollins was getting real flak off The Shed, and the whole Chelsea thing was massive, even though we were struggling.'

'They moved me in to temporary digs in Hayes – next door was Mick Bodley's parents. He was at Chelsea too. I had been in one of the dodgy Kensington hotels and was glad to get out of there. I had to settle down fast. I kept in touch with Susan, the plan being for us to get a place somewhere in London in time. But a lot was happening fast; I bought myself an A-reg Escort and drove to the training ground each day. Training was good – Chelsea had a lot of coaches and I generally trained with all the 'keepers, and there was quite a few there. Eddie Niedzwiecki and Tony Godden were brilliant to me, and helped me settle in quickly. There was a strict training regime, but by 12.30 each day we were finished. Sometimes I would stay on and work on my game, just me and Glen Hoddle, who was getting fit after an injury sustained in Monaco, knocking the ball about, but generally you would have the afternoons free to play snooker or relax. A good life eh? But of course at the time you didn't realise it, and like all things it got me down. My family were hundreds of miles away, they may have been in Italy as Newport, and at times it was lonely. I was playing in the Combination League for the reserves, and didn't really think I would get a first-team game for a few seasons. To be truthful now, if that was to be the case I don't think I would have stayed at the club for as long as I did.'

'The fans at Chelsea are very demanding, you only had to look around the training ground to see how much pressure was on people. The hallways of Stamford Bridge were littered with the glory years of Osgood, Webb, Houseman, Hollins and Hudson – the real Chelsea folklore players. It was daunting. They were once European Cup winners, FA Cup winners and League Champions. This team, the team I was now a part of, had beaten Real Madrid in a European final. If I dwelt upon it too much I would have gone mad. The supporters had a bad reputation, but like all football fans they were friendly and interested in you as a person. And for that reason alone I wanted to do well for them – and some of them are the reason why I just love to play the game. I had been at the club for no more than six weeks when I was selected to play for the first team against QPR. Now this was a real chance. My dad was so excited, and I could see he was really proud of me. This was going to be so different to playing for County that was for sure.'

'I made my debut in April 1987. The astroturf thing was big at the time, and Loftus Road was one of the pitches that had the stuff in abundance. It was really odd playing on it, and I was so nervous that I was to make my debut for the club on such an unpredictable surface. The club had a goalkeeping crisis, and I was the answer. We drew that game 1-1 and afterwards I was just happy to say I had not been on the losing side. That night I drove home back to Newport to be with the family – the next day being a Sunday I felt that I deserved the night with my folks. It was a bad move. The next morning I should have been in training at 11 a.m. I left

Newport early, in time to get to the training ground in London. By the time I hit the M4 (literally) at Magor, I had written off my Escort and nearly myself. It was silly to even think I could rush down to Wales and then back to Chelsea for the Sunday morning session. One minute I was travelling along in Old Faithful, the next I was smashing into the motorway barrier and spinning out of control. I had a blow out which totalled my car completely. Being a careful Welshman, I had only insured my car third party: it cost me £1,500 to pay for the barrier repairs, and of course I was without a car. But I was okay. Back then mobile phones were not as available as they are now, and I would have needed a trailer to carry it in they were that big. I couldn't get hold of John Hollins, and by the time my train pulled in to Paddington it was 9 p.m.'

'I sensed I was in trouble, but when I explained what had happened John Hollins just asked me if I was okay, which I was. He then said I was playing against Leicester in a few days time. I got away with no fine, which in the circumstances was right, and I had kept my place in the side. For the rest of the season I kept my place. We beat Leicester 3-1, lost 2-1 at Wimbledon and 1-0 to Newcastle. We managed draws against Southampton, and I had a belter of a game against Liverpool which we drew 3-3. That was Ian Rush's last game for the club before he went to Juventus, and it was on the television too. The season ended and we had managed to stay up, but I felt that John Hollins could go at anytime. Ken Bates wanted success and we all knew how much the club meant to him. I knew that if Hollins failed the next season he would be sacked. Maybe I was getting a bit of my dad's intuition, but Chelsea was and still is a massive club. Failure is not on the agenda.'

'In March I was playing for Newport County in front of a few thousand against Chesterfield. In April I was playing in front of a full house against Liverpool. Jimmy Greaves was right, it is indeed a funny old game. But at times I failed to see the funny side. The pressure was immense and when the season ended I was relieved. It wouldn't be the last time I would be relieved for a game or a season to end, it was nice to know that for a few weeks there would be no more pressure, and I could go back to being a teenager,'

'Summer is a strange time for a professional footballer. Some go on the lash for a few months and knock out their fitness in a few weeks before pre-season, some stay with their families. I went home to Newport and worked in a sports shop for £30 a week. I didn't need the money, but I am one of those people who always needs to be doing something. Hyperactive maybe? I went to work at John Macey's shop in Chepstow Road, Newport. He was the reserve team manager at Newport then and was a goalkeeper too. He had taught me a lot during my time at Newport and I was happy to potter away in the shop during the day and spend the nights with Susan. It was a good time for a lot of reasons, but I did feel a sense of loss that I was to go back to London in a few weeks and prepare for a big season at Chelsea. I have to say it wasn't the club, but that pressure which I keep referring to – that sort of pressure in a job at nineteen is not good for you. Football is a very insecure employment. I found that out at Newport. One minute you are flavour of the day, the next you are on your arse – quite literally. It is never constant, you rely on others for your well-being and future development, and that is one of the things which is bad in football. There are people in the game who will shaft you for no other reason than they can, or they want to. Chelsea would turn out to be no different in time, but I had a big duty to their army of proud supporters and I was determined to do my best. John Hollins seemed relaxed enough during pre-season, but I still had this sense that he would not be at the club for long if we faltered – more pressure, and unnecessary pressure at that, for me as a player. But of course, it was me who was putting myself under pressure, nobody else.'

'We started the 1987/88 season with Eddie Niedzwiecki as first-choice 'keeper. As is traditional with 'keepers, he got injured in his first game back. That left me, as number two, to stand in for him. I came back for the 3-1 defeat at Arsenal. I remember Roy Wegerle was through on goal for us when it was 1-1, when for some reason he blasted the ball into the crowd and stopped when it would have been easier to score. I couldn't work that one out at all, why did he do that? The manager asked him the same question at half time. Roy said he thought he had been blown up by the ref for being offside. The fact was that someone in the crowd had done the ref's job for him. Roy stopped, and signalled his disgust by blasting the ball into the crowd. The ref asked him what he was playing at and Roy immediately realised what he had done. People say that seasons turn on certain incidents, and for me this was one of them. If he had gone on to score who knows what would have happened. The fact was we went on a miserable run of defeats and I was custodian for all of them. My worst fears became reality when Ken Bates decided he had enough of John Hollins and sacked him. I remember feeling a bit lost at the time, after all John had brought me to the club – well, in a roundabout way, I'm unsure to be honest if he had much to do with the initial scouting and dealings, but he was the manager. And for a young player, playing in a losing team it was blow. But that's being selfish; we had a job to do and were failing badly. The truth is we were staring at relegation and going through the motions. Ken Bates had no choice but to sack him, and John Hollins was in a rut at the club, even I could see that. We were losing because of a lack of training methods, and the players felt we were rudderless. John resented Bobby Campbell being brought in too, as I did. He was a horrible man, who was rude and arrogant to players and very cutting in his remarks to us. I remember once after a training session he called me a "wanker". I could have knocked him down there and then, but I just replied "Is that all I am today boss?" The rest of the players laughed, but I could see from the look on his face he didn't like me, and the feeling was very mutual, I hated him.

'Bobby Campbell was a family friend of Ken Bates, a blustering man who seemed to enjoy making people feel useless – some would say it was a way of motivating players, I would say it was a good way of going about getting a hiding. These days I wouldn't put up with it, but back then I was a young man making his way in the game. I gave him a few words back now and again, but on the whole I just resented him totally. And many of the younger players felt the same way. With leadership like that the only way was down. John Hollins had laid the foundations for relegation, but Bobby Campbell took us there. On the other hand I liked Ken Bates a lot. He may not have a massive Christmas card collection, but he was a one-hundred-per-cent Chelsea fan. He had good vision about the way football was going, and he knew what he wanted. He has a love-hate relationship with the Chelsea fans, but you only have to look at what he has achieved at Chelsea to see he was right and his vision served them well. He never suffered fools gladly, and that is why he is a success. Okay, you will earn few friends when you take this path, but Chelsea needed him at the time, and they needed his ideas. Look at Chelsea today, it's not only a football club it's an empire, a Ken Bates empire. Hotels, shops and commercial activity on a level only a few clubs enjoy. His drive and enthusiasm is the reason for that in my opinion, and the FA have made a drastic error in not having him involved at the highest level with the new Wembley. They left it to politicians who have no clue about football and administrators who have no business sense. When I look at our own National Stadium in Cardiff, it makes me think that not everything is wrong with the Welsh game. And anyway, where are they playing the FA Cup finals for the next few years? It's a sad day when an FA as big as England's can't get it together to build a stadium like ours. And an even sadder one that personality conflicts affect such ventures. Ken Bates has a massive personality, but he also has football at heart – love him or loathe him, I don't think Chelsea would be half the club they are now without him. Justification of this can be seen when you see how long Bobby Campbell lasted at Chelsea after the slump. Not long at all – and rightly so.

'Something that will always stay with me about Ken Bates was the time I was given a new Chelsea contract. I was not on a lot at the time, and we had just been promoted back to the First Division. Ken Bates got me in to his office, and I will admit it now I was in awe of him. He is a big figure in the game, always with a view and an opinion, and I was just Roger Freestone. He looked at me and winked. "I'm about to make you a very rich man" he said. "Christ" I thought, "I've arrived at last". I had visions of driving home in a brand new Mercedes car, and being able to buy a bigger house, all sorts of things. I signed the contract and felt on top of the world. When I analysed it later I noticed he had given me a £50 a week pay rise! Trust me, that takes a few years to laugh about afterwards, but I do now. He is a mercurial figure, one of the game's real assets, and when it all worked out I was on £550 a week, so why should I care? That's not a bad wage for a twenty-year-old for playing football every week. Many people have said to me that I have been stupid with my football career, but I don't think so. Okay, I could have gone anywhere at one time or another, but I find it hard not to be loyal. There are many who will smile in your face and then stab you in the back, but I am trusting and I want to do my best as a footballer while I can. That's why I am at the level I am with Swansea City, and that's why I sweated a lot over my game at Chelsea. I wanted to succeed and be thought of as a nice person. For me the life of Ken Bates is not the one I want to live. But football needs characters like him, and players like me need characters like him. It makes us believe.'

With Eddie Niedzwiecki out injured, Roger now found himself the regular Chelsea goalkeeper. After presiding over a number of defeats, the Chelsea support were quick to criticise him. Eddie stood firm alongside Roger and spoke out against the critics, 'Roger has done very, very well, and shown a lot of character. It's been a trial for him, and he has taken some unkind criticism, but he has realised that you are there to be shot at and hopefully he will keep improving.' These were kind words from Chelsea's first choice 'keeper, and Roger was keen not only to hear them, but to have someone around him being supportive. It was a hard time. Roger also had another agenda. He wanted to secure the appearances that were needed to help his ailing hometown club, Newport County. £20,000 would go Newport's way if he made twenty first-team games, with a further £20,000 if he made forty appearances. Roger was heard making that point at every interview he did, 'There is a terrible air of depression about Newport, and I just want to get the cash for them, so it helps them out, I know I was lucky to leave when I did, but they need the money. And I can get it for them.' Newport County was never far from Roger's thoughts, and this was the only way he could repay them. However, he was still having his own problems with the fans at Chelsea. The turning point was a game at Derby County in January 1988, when Roger saved a penalty from John Gregory (now the manager of Aston Villa). The Blues went on to earn a good 3-1 away win, Kerry Dixon – an England international forward who was rated as being worth £2 million – earning all three points.

The next match was at Old Trafford for a FA Cup fixture against Manchester United, under the eye of manager Alex Ferguson. Although Chelsea lost the game 2-0, Roger was again hailed as a hero and made man of the match, after wonderfully saving Brian McClair's penalty. After the game, Hollins was being stubborn with the press and refused to comment on his managerial future at Stamford Bridge – something that Ken Bates would decide upon in the very near future. Many people disagreed with his team selections, with Steve Bruce, the United captain, joining in the criticism of the Chelsea manager. Manchester United had worked all week on closing down and dealing with Chelsea's flair player, Mickey Hazard. Hollins didn't give him a start, which surprised even Bruce. Hazard had looked good alongside Pat Nevin and Kerry Dixon, and his non-inclusion infuriated even the most patient of Chelsea fans.

Nigel Clough turned the screw on Chelsea's season when he contributed to a 3-2 Forest win a week later, leaving Chelsea's position in the First Division looking precarious. Another penalty was awarded against Chelsea in this game and Roger came within an inch of saving Clough's spot kick. The inevitable conclusion to an interesting and exciting season for Roger was relegation, something he took very personally indeed.

'The relegation season at Chelsea was hard to take. Bobby Campbell clearly didn't like me and I found myself dropped to number three. Perry Digweed had arrived on loan and Kevin Hitchcock was signed from Mansfield. Perry was a good 'keeper at times, and Kevin's arrival meant I was in the South East Counties League with the pressure right off me. Whilst in the third team as such, I realised just how intense the whole situation had been. I wasn't too worried, but like any player it wasn't where I wanted to be. It gave me time though to assess where I was, and Susan had moved to London so we could live together. After the relegation I was hurting a lot, and Susan was not happy.

'We had moved to Reading to be together, so I thought it was the right time to get married. But there was no way I was getting married in Reading. Susan hated the place, and she had very few friends there. As much as she could she would travel back to Newport to be with her family, and I don't blame her at all. We decided to set a date to get married – 18 June 1988 at St Mary's Church in Risca. John, my brother, was to be my best man. God knows, thinking back, how Susan put up with it all. She was a bit older than me, but is very much a family person, and being in Reading when everyone you know and love is in Gwent is hard.

Susan Freestone takes up the story. 'I had known Roger for years and years. We first met as kids just messing about in the street, as you do when you are young. My boyfriend at the time was a boy called Chris James – he was one of Roger's best mates. So Chris wasn't very happy when I started going out with Roger. He shouldn't have introduced us should he?' Susan laughs, 'Roger was very different from other boys. He looked after you very well indeed, from day one he has been a very caring partner, and I wouldn't be without him. When we met I was fifteen and Roger was thirteen, he was my toy boy. The thing that struck you about him then was how tall he was. He had very curly hair with a middle parting, and was football mad. He would train every Tuesday and Thursday, play every Saturday and Sunday, and the rest of the time we just used to hang about together. That was our life, football and being together, and nothing much has changed. Even when he was at Newport he was the same person I knew when we were kids, just a very caring man. But he tore my life apart when he signed for Chelsea. He told me he wouldn't do it, I thought he would keep his word, but only afterwards did he tell me. That absolutely destroyed me. He signed for Chelsea on my birthday, 9 March 1987. "Happy birthday Susan" I thought. I thought I had lost him forever. It was a testing time for us. I don't think his dad wanted him to sign for Chelsea, but when you think about it now you can't blame him when he did. I still say it was a big mistake, but then again I wasn't thinking about football, I was thinking about me and Roger. We looked all over for a house we could afford and in the end we bought a house in Reading. We moved to 48 Sweetbriar Drive in Calcot, Reading, and I hated it. I knew nobody at all. I spent a lot of time on the motorway going home, that's where I wanted to be. The house cost us £60,000 and was very nice, but you can only like a house for so long, you need more than that. After Chelsea were relegated, Roger and I decided to get married. It was a good thing we did too. I needed something to occupy my mind, something to look forward to. We had a family holiday in Ibiza, and Roger was out of control at times. He has never been a big drinker, but one night I thought he would kill himself. He drunk so much he couldn't speak or walk properly. We went back to our apartment which was five floors up, and I thought he had fallen off the balcony. He was going to the toilet off the balcony, shouting and singing away and I couldn't get him in. He fell forward and I thought he had gone over. I was terrified, but the next thing I knew he was back up, God knows how, and looking for our dog Sandy. He was very drunk – the dog bit was my fault though, I told him the dog had flown over to see him, just to get him off the balcony. Yes, Roger can be a bit mad at times, but you can't help loving him for it. But he knows as well as everyone else that I wanted him to leave Chelsea from day one; I was too young, he was too young, and I felt helpless up there on my own.'

Susan's mother, Sheila, confirms just how unhappy her daughter was. 'God, she would cry to me on the phone, and that made me sad because I knew that the pair of them were very happy together, it was just that Susan hated it in Reading. Even though she was with Roger, they weren't if you know what I mean. His football took him away a lot, and Susan would be on her own up there, and it was quite away from London anyway. She would come home as much as she could, and Roger would too, just to be together. It was a very hard time for them as a young couple, but I knew even though this Reading thing was difficult them that they would pull through. You only have to know Roger to know he would do the right thing. I know if he had to he would have packed in football if it meant keeping Susan happy. Not that any of us expected him to do that at all. He was very young, but even as a teenager when we first met him he was a very nice person, he would call round most days to see Susan, and it was quite a way away from his home, and that caused him problems in itself.'

Roger's father-in-law, Ivor, remembers the times Roger had to fight for his life because he was going out with a Risca girl and not from the area. 'He would come up most days, but the local lads hated him because he was from Rogerstone. They would pick fights with him because of it. It got so bad he used to carry a hammer up his sleeve to protect himself when he was attacked. He would have to run all the way home, but I bet that kept him fit. Good training in a way. It's funny now when you look back, Roger having to dodge his way home because the local boys wanted to fight him. But he wasn't a fighter then, and anyone will tell you that at thirteen and fourteen he wasn't a big lad at all. He shot up to over six foot when he hit sixteen, but initially he was a small lad. He would prefer the quiet life, but football has brought something out of him that is honourable. He doesn't prop up bars or nothing, and in the football season you don't see him with an alcoholic drink, he would rather come straight back home after training than hang about in Swansea doing the "Big I Am" thing. That's the fighter he is now – he can turn his back on all the razzmatazz easily, he doesn't need it. I should think that any manager would be pleased to have such a solid man like that in his side. But yes, they were not very happy in Reading, and they were young. I expected it really, but they knew where they could come to get some peace and be with friends and family, not that it affected Roger's playing side. I was very proud to see him on the TV playing for Chelsea, but away from that it was clear they had things to sort out.'

Roger was a young man waiting to get married, in turmoil over a relegation and with a fiancée unhappy with her domestic situation. You would have thought would affect a young professional's game, but he dealt with it much in the same way as he did when he learned he could go to Manchester United. 'Basically, I thought "sod it". I knew we were to be in the Second Division, but I also felt we would bounce straight back up. Maybe that was the arrogant side of me, but I knew we would do it, even with Bobby Campbell.'

'I was playing regularly with Chelsea, and the Second Division was a lot easier for us. But I knew that Susan was unhappy, and that bothered me a lot. I played quite regularly that season. Chelsea was fine, it was just all the stuff going on away from there. The playing staff was great, people like Kerry Dixon, Pat Nevin, John Bumstead, Colin Pates and Dave Beasant – who had been signed from Newcastle too. We were winning lots of games and the feel-good factor was great. It's hard to explain, but I was playing in a winning side and looking at some end-of-season honours. That's a real result when you are nineteen or twenty years of age. I had a magnificent house in Reading too, but that's where the problems started, Sue hated it.'

On the pitch, the season back in the Second Division was easier for Roger, in fact he even found himself enjoying the thought of playing for Chelsea. The nerves were going, and he was becoming more experienced. The Blues, who were 5/1 promotion favourites to win the division, made a faltering start. Gordon Durie was the man with the responsibility of scoring the goals as, surprisingly, Dixon had failed to find the net in ten months for the club. Roger found himself starting games and, although he made a glaring error at Selhurst Park against Crystal Palace, it would later be seen as a blatant push on him by Palace striker Mark Bright. Chelsea kept in contention during the early months without setting the world alight, and were whacked 4-1 by Scunthorpe United in the League Cup, Roger making an error for number three after pulling off an inital superb save. Plymouth were despatched 5-0 at The Bridge, but Hull City took Chelsea apart for their first win over the London club in fifty-three years and denied Bobby Campbell five League wins out of five for the month of October. Statistics show Roger hitting marks of 7 and 8 out of 10 for his performances, and a report of an away game at Stoke City in December, which Chelsea won 3-0, refers to him as a world class goalkeeper with a massive future. Roger's success between the sticks when facing penalties continued, with another memorable moment against Oxford United. This contribution, and many world class saves, saw Chelsea to a championship win, albeit over lesser opposition than Chelsea had been previously used to. But the Second Division was there to be won, and Roger played a massive part in Chelsea's return to the top flight.

Roger was championship winner with Chelsea, but the club's promotion back to the top flight brought with it some new difficulties. 'That was a real problem, getting promoted. It may sound odd, but Dave Beasant was now with us, and Kevin Hitchcock was back to fitness – I was, in fact, Chelsea's number three, having played and been involved in the promotion a few months before. It should have raised alarm bells for me really, but I battled on. There was a few loan deals, of course, to Swansea and also Hereford United, but I wanted away. It came home to me after Ian Evans had signed me on loan for three months to Swansea. I just wanted to get back to Wales, to be with my family and for Susan to be happy. I was at a crossroads.'

Roger just before playing for Chelsea at Stamford Bridge.

Roger wears the number one Chelsea jersey with pride.

Roger at the Chelsea training ground.

Roger just prior to his Chelsea debut, on the astroturf at QPR.

Above and below: Roger at his Chelsea training sessions.

Roger joins the big guns at Chelsea. He is standing at the right end of the back row. Kerry Dixon is also on the back row (fourth from the right) and Roy Wegerle is next to him. Also on the back row (extreme left) is Eddie Nziedzwiecki. In the middle row, Gordon Durie is fifth from the right and Tony Dorigo third from the right, with John Bumstead next to him. Pat Nevin is on the far left of the front row, with John Hollins in the centre and Micky Hazard – the player Manchester United were determined to mark out of the game he never started – also on the front row, second from the right. Next to Hazard is Kevin Wilson, who went on to play for and manage Northampton Town.

4

MOVING ON AGAIN

Roger's career at Chelsea was heading nowhere as the 1989/90 season began. He was third in the pecking order, with Dave Beasant the man in possession that both Roger and Kevin Hitchcock had to edge out of the side. Beasant had been a member of the Wimbledon side that had defeated Liverpool in the FA Cup final and was enjoying a superb spell between the sticks, while Roger and Hitchcock alternated between performances in the reserves.

Life was not happy for the Freestone family at this time. Both Roger and Susan were miserable in their Reading home and homesick for friends and family back in Wales. Reserve team football was not what Roger wanted at this time, and this was compounded by an unhappy relationship with his manager, Bobby Campbell. Roger was keen to move on, the only question that needed answering was who wanted him?

The answer was to come a few weeks into the season when Ian Evans, manager of Swansea City, approached Chelsea to see if they would release Roger on loan for three months. Swansea were enjoying their second season back in the Third Division, having scaled the dizzy heights of the First less than ten years before. Lee Bracey was their first choice goalkeeper, but was going through a bad patch, and had conceded five in his previous appearance. Roger could not believe his luck that, just as he was wishing to move on, a club so close to his 'home' in Risca wanted to secure his services.

He agreed to the loan proposal without hesitation, and arrangements were quickly made for him to move in with Susan's mother back in Risca whilst playing at Swansea. Roger signed his three-month contract on 28 September 1989 and was immediately introduced to his team-mates, including future Welsh internationals Andy Melville and Chris Coleman, and was straight into the side for the next game, against Notts County at The Vetch. Swansea drew 0-0 and Roger was back in action with a clean sheet to start what was to become a long love affair with Swansea City. Also included in the Swansea line-up that day was the local home-grown talent of Andy Legg and Simon Davey.

As far as Roger was concerned, Ian Evans, the Swansea manager, was a complete contrast to Bobby Campbell. Evans was very approachable, and Roger still believes to this day that he was treated badly at Swansea, being forced out when Terry Yorath returned from an unsuccessful spell at Bradford.

That first appearance between the sticks at The Vetch was the first of a series of clean sheet victories, removing the gloom that had hung over the Swansea faithful – before Roger's arrival, a run of defeats had left them near the foot of the Third Division. It was returning home in more ways than one, as it meant a reunion with a face from his Newport County days, Terry Boyle. Terry had joined Swansea from rivals Cardiff City that season (making a rare treble in Welsh football ranks). A tough, no-nonsense defender, Boyle was also a very likeable person, and Roger happily agreed to drive via Cardiff every morning to pick him up and transport him to the Vetch.

These were happy times for Roger. He was back in Wales and back in regular football action as Swansea gained some very credible results. It is with great fondness that Roger remembers one game in particular against Bristol City at Ashton Gate. This was the next best thing to a Welsh derby, against a side flying high in the Third Division, and something that the players looked forward to.

Swansea had secured the services of a young John Salako from Crystal Palace on loan and he was included in the squad that made the short trip over the Severn Bridge, followed by several hundred supporters making the journey. Swansea made a dream start to the game and were two goals to the good, with Salako tearing the home side to pieces with attacking runs and accurate passing. The Swansea fans behind the Freestone goal were in full voice – something that Roger was experiencing for the first time. The inspiring noise coming from the terraces made him realise what such passionate support could do for the relative underdog.

Swansea eventually won the game 3-1, Salako scoring twice, and it was a happy journey back into South Wales with the three points safely in the bag. During Roger's time on loan, Swansea successfully negotiated the first two rounds of the FA Cup and landed a plum third-round home tie against holders Liverpool. Sadly, Roger knew it was not going to be a game that he would be able to take part in, his three-month loan spell ending beforehand and, unless a permanent move was in the offing, then he would be back at Stamford Bridge when the fixture came around.

One of Swansea's most popular players of this era was Tommy Hutchinson. Hutchinson was in his forties, but still capable of taking on defenders half his age and the supporters loved to see nothing better than the lanky Scotsman gliding down the left wing with the ball apparently tied to his foot. Hutchinson was to put in class performances against some of Europe's biggest teams during his time with the Swans, although he was known throughout football for an unusual feat back in 1981. Then in the Manchester City side, he scored one of the best diving headers ever seen at Wembley. Manchester City were still a goal up well into the second half when he deflected a free-kick into the back of his own net for the equaliser. The game eventually ended 1-1, with Hutchinson the scorer at both ends. City eventually lost the replay, but this game placed Tommy Hutchinson's name in the history of the FA Cup forever.

There was another side to Hutchinson not apparent to those outside football, but it was one that Roger had heard of at close hand and one that he didn't want to see. Tommy was a great believer that you became a better footballer the harder you worked. He did not agree with the methods of Ian Evans and and demonstrated this to all the players. Hutchinsion was determined to stamp his mark on the team, and did so in a way that Roger was not prepared for. Because of his experience at the highest level, Hutchinson must have found the drop in the standard of football a struggle, which at times rubbed off on the other players. Youngsters like Andrew Melville and Chris Coleman were tutored forcibly by Hutchinson, and his techniques for grooming these young players were at times bought into question. Suffice to say both Melville and Coleman have succeeded at the highest level in British football, although whether this is because of or in spite of Hutchinson's methods is open to speculation, both players being apparently reluctant to talk about their time with Swansea City.

Despite tensions like these, Roger enjoyed this brief period with Swansea immensely and was saddened when it came to an end. The loan spell ended with the fixture that Swansea fans hold in the highest regard of all, Cardiff City visiting Vetch Field on Boxing Day 1989. People from all over Britain talk about rivalry games and which is the biggest – but for people in South Wales, nothing is more intense than Swansea City *v*. Cardiff City.

A crowd of 13,000 abandoned their cold turkey for the derby game. Nothing had prepared Roger for the spectacle of that day. It hit him as he entered the field of play from the tunnel to be greeted with a cauldron of noise and mass of colour – white one side and blue the other. The Swansea support was boosted by the fact that the club were offering vouchers for the upcoming Liverpool game with the matchday programme, and this helped generate the charged atmosphere that was to live with Roger when he headed back to London.

It was clear from the intensity of the support that winning meant everything to both sets of fans, and would far outweigh anything that Father Christmas had delivered the day before. It was, sadly for Roger, to prove an unfortunate end to his loan spell as the Bluebirds went home happy thanks to a Leigh Barnard goal which gave them a 1-0 victory. Immediately after the conclusion of the match, Roger appealed to the Chelsea board to release him from his contract, but they refused.

Swansea made a further move to sign Roger on a permanent basis on New Year's Eve, offering Chelsea £100,000 to secure his services. However, Bobby Campbell refused to release Roger from his contract, a move that Roger still believes was partly due to the mutual dislike the two men had for each other. So it was back up to London for Roger and another spell in Chelsea reserves as he contemplated his future. It was during the next few months that Roger started to question whether he had a football career in front of him or not. Three months of regular first-team football had whetted his appetite again, and sitting in the reserves at Chelsea was not how he had pictured his career developing when he left Newport County three years previous.

Roger and Susan were still unhappy in their Reading home and wanted to move back to Wales. The news that Susan was expecting their first child only fuelled that desire, and Roger began to look around for jobs outside football to support his wife and their unborn baby. Applications were placed in various outlets in Wales for work but nothing came from them and the only hope for Roger was a transfer out of London. Hartlepool came in for him, offering a three-month loan spell which Chelsea agreed to release Roger for. As he was homesick for Wales, a few months in the North East did not appeal to Roger and he refused the move, worsening the relationship between himself and Campbell.

The future was a regular topic of conversation between Roger and Susan, and they both agreed that they wanted their first child to be born on Welsh soil. Consequently, Susan moved back to live with her parents while Roger spent all his free time with her whilst continuing his spells in the reserves. Hereford United provided a release from this hell for Roger as they came in with the offer of a loan move on transfer deadline day in 1990. As with the previous loan to South Wales, Roger had no hesitation in accepting the proposal, delighted by the fact that he would be closer to home and able to see more of his family and friends.

His debut came two days later against Scarborough, and Roger was once again playing in the Football League. It was particularly important to him to be close to Susan at this time, as she was experiencing problems with the pregnancy and he felt more comfortable being on hand to provide support. Ian Bowyer, a former European Cup winner with Nottingham Forest, was in charge at Edgar Street and again Roger found himself working under a completely different regime to that he had been used to at Chelsea. Tony Elliott, the incumbent Hereford goalkeeper, had been going through a rough period of form and Bowyer was looking for the 'keeper to replace him. Roger fitted the bill and found himself enjoying life at Hereford.

Although a fair manager, Bowyer also had a tough streak, which reflected in the way he had played his football, but Roger felt that his career was progressing nicely. Off the pitch, however, a worrying period was just around the corner. The day before a game against Exeter in Hereford, Bowyer had decided that his team should spend the day and night before the game in a hotel. As Roger joined the rest of the squad, a call came in from Risca to say that Susan had been rushed into hospital, bleeding heavily. Only four months pregnant at the time, Roger knew that this could be serious, but due to problems with his previous management he worried what the reaction of Ian Bowyer would be if he left the squad.

He needn't have been concerned, as Bowyer fully appreciated his decision and instructed him to go home and report for the match the next day. Thankfully, Susan recovered completely, and Roger was able to travel back up to Hereford the next day, safe in the knowledge that the panic was over and duly able to take his place between the sticks for another Freestone-inspired victory. Roger saw out the rest of the season with Hereford, but no permanent move evolved, with cash clearly an issue, and he spent the summer again contemplating his future, knowing that he would not be first choice at Chelsea.

The close season passed and, with Susan's pregnancy showing more and more, Roger returned to London and pre-season training at Stamford Bridge. With Dave Beasant still the first choice 'keeper, Roger knew that he was going to alternate in the reserves with Kevin Hitchcock. Although Hitchcock seemed content with this arrangement, it was not what Roger wanted and he still yearned for a move away from Stamford Bridge, preferably closer to home.

In the early hours of 30 August 1990, Roger underwent an experience that changed his life forever. For once, it had nothing to do with football. He was living in digs nearer to Chelsea's ground while Susan lived with her parents in Risca. Roger travelled back home on days off and, on this particular Wednesday, events determined that Roger had a few more days off than expected. Susan's waters broke in the evening and the Freestones made their way to the Royal Gwent hospital for the birth. Roger did not leave Susan's side during the night as the labour progressed and, just before 8 a.m. the following morning, Daniel Leigh came into the world weighing 8lb 3oz.

As the midwife turned to Roger and pronounced that it was a boy, emotion overcame the strapping goalkeeper and he broke down in tears of joy at the birth of his first child. It was with great pride that Roger did the duty bestowed upon the father and rang first Susan's parents, immediately followed by his own. One of the biggest surprises in the days that followed the birth was a big bouquet of flowers from the Chelsea chairman, Ken Bates, which arrived in Wales soon after, showing a sensitive side to the man that people outside Chelsea Football Club very rarely see.

Roger was given the rest of the week and the weekend off to help settle in with the baby and – although living with Susan's parents was not an ideal situation – mother and baby returned home the following Saturday. The birth of Daniel only increased Roger's desire to leave Chelsea and the Freestones started to make preparations to buy a house in Risca and move home on a permanent basis.

The joy of the birth of Daniel was tinged with sadness, because Roger was forced to spend so much time during the week in London, even though he was only festering in the reserves. This arrangement was to continue for another year, as no club appeared to be interested in making a bid for Roger. He spent the next twelve months between his two residences, and yet again thoughts that he might have to make a life outside football started entering his head.

After the close of the 1990/91 season, Roger spent the summer with Susan and Daniel and they moved into their new house. A young family, with the husband in a job that he is not enjoying is not a particularly unusual situation and they began to assess their options for the future. As the summer came to an end, Roger returned for another round of pre-season training to prepare for another season in the reserves with little or no chance of first-team football. Chelsea had appointed a new manager, with Ian Porterfield taking over from Bobby Campbell. Although, this improved the situation for Roger, it was still clear that there was no future for him at Stamford Bridge. Relief was, however, just around the corner and for the second time in a little more over twelve months, a life-changing event was not far away.

A Friday morning training session at Chelsea had just finished when Roger was called into see Ian Porterfield and Stan Ternant (now manager of Burnley). They told Roger that a club had come in for him and asked if he would he be interested in moving on. Of course Roger was interested, but the last thing he wanted was a club further away from home. It was with a sense of disbelief that he heard that the team in question was Swansea City. Swansea was less than 60 miles from Risca, which meant he could move back in with his family on a permanent basis. Without hesitation, Roger agreed to the transfer. He could have punched the air with joy and relief – not only was his career back on track, but it was at a place where he had experienced three happy months less than two years previously.

Roger had to wait to break the news to Susan, as Swansea wanted to see him immediately so that they could register the transfer before the 5 p.m. Football League deadline in order for him to play for them at Fulham the next day. A hotel in Reading was the venue for the meeting with Swansea City representatives, who finalised the details of the transfer. Like the last time, this was initially to be a three-month loan spell. However, this time was different in that Chelsea had agreed that if things were to work out in Swansea there would be a permanent move at the end of it. Roger was not particularly bothered about this, he was just happy at being back in Wales again.

He rang Susan and told her that a club had come in for him. At first she gave a subdued response as the same thoughts that had passed through his own mind passed through hers. Which club? Would it mean moving again? Would she see less of Roger than she did now? When Roger revealed it was Swansea she was overjoyed. Roger explained the terms of the three-month loan with a move to permanent transfer. Both of them realised that this was almost beyond their wildest dreams. Susan was slightly apprehensive just in case it didn't work out at The Vetch, but Roger told her that he would make certain that it did and that in three months time he would be a Swansea City player.

Roger was to make his debut the following day at Fulham. Frank Burrows, a tough talking Scot, was in charge of Swansea, but Roger did not meet him until the following day on the team bus. They shared a conversation that Friday evening and Burrows scared the life out of Roger with his broad Scottish accent and direct talking, although he realised that he owed Frank a big vote of thanks for reviving his career. The next day, Roger pulled on the Swans number one jersey and made his debut in a 3-0 reverse at Fulham – not the best start when you are trying to impress and get a permanent move. However, as he headed back to Wales on the team bus, Roger reflected on a reasonable performance, despite the goals conceded, and looked forward to spending time in his house with his wife and young son.

On loan again and on duty with Wales under-21s at Somerton Park, Newport.

On loan at Swansea City.

5

COMING HOME

Finally, Roger was back in Wales and determined to make the most of his new opportunity. Swansea is around 50 miles west of Newport, where it had all begun with his debut less than five years before. Although he had enjoyed his time at Chelsea initially, the final couple of years under Bobby Campbell were not at all what he had wanted. This escape was welcome relief for Roger, and he was determined that it would work for him.

It was good to be back home with Susan and Dan and, as far as he was concerned, Swansea City could have been the worst club in the world – it would not have made any difference to his decision after thoughts of quitting football and finding a job elsewhere during the darkest days. Ironically, it was probably ignoring some advice from his father, Eddie, that stopped him finding a job outside football during those bleak final months at Chelsea. All through Roger's childhood, Eddie had impressed on him to finish his exams and not concentrate all his efforts into making it as a professional. Roger had, as most people in his position probably would have done, ignored that advice, and to this day he regrets not heeding those words. Had he have followed them, Welsh football could have been deprived of one of its best players.

Things worked out for Roger at Swansea more quickly than he could have hoped for. Despite that opening defeat at Fulham, he displaced Mark Kendall (again) between the sticks to become the first choice goalkeeper for Frank Burrows. Roger had again teamed up with Mark, who lived in Blackwood (a small village not far from Roger's home in Risca), to share lifts into Swansea on a daily basis. Roger had always respected Mark as a player and, despite the professional competition, they got on well and helped each other's game. Kendall would eventually leave football and take up a career in the police service.

In 1990/91, Swansea enjoyed several tilts at big opposition in various cup competitions. As Welsh Cup holders, they were competing in the Cup Winners Cup and had drawn Monaco. To add to the excitement, two weeks before the fixture against the crack French side, Swansea were due to play the mighty Tottenham Hotspur, the FA Cup holders, at the Vetch for a Rumbelows Cup tie. Swansea had, in the week been leading up to the game, tried on several occasions to agree terms with Roger. They wanted to make the move permanent, and press reports suggested that both sides were struggling to agree personal terms. Chelsea were refusing to let Roger play in the match. They argued that they did not want him cup-tied in case the deal did not work out. It was a frustrating situation for Roger, as he had been playing well and did not want to miss out.

Frank Burrows realised this and also wanted Roger to play. He persuaded the Swansea board that this was their man and decided that they would register him as a permanent player that day to enable him to play in the game. The transfer was completed just hours before the Tottenham game started for a deal that amounted to just less than £50,000. Roger, like quite a few of the Swansea professionals, was scared stiff of Frank Burrows. Frank had the no-nonsense approach of not negotiating new contracts. Players were told what was on offer and they either signed it or they didn't – it was as simple as that. His job was football management and the less time that he could spend negotiating new deals the better. Roger's offer was laid on the table for him early that afternoon and, although it was a drop in wages from what he had been earning at Chelsea, it was again without hesitation that he signed the contract, severing all ties with Stamford Bridge.

Although Mark Kendall had expected to play, it was Roger that was going to line up in front of a full Vetch Field against the FA Cup holders. Mark accepted Frank's decision and wished Roger all the best in the game, his first as a full-time Swansea City player. All the talk around the Vetch Field amongst the supporters was of a game that had taken place over twelve years earlier in the same competition. At that time, Tottenham had signed Osvaldo Ardiles, a World Cup-winning Argentinian international and were expected to win comfortably. Ardiles had been welcomed to The Vetch by Swansea midfielder Tommy Smith, whose tackle sent him up in the air and rattled the whole Tottenham team. Although that game had ended as a draw, Swansea had won the replay in one of their most famous victories of all time. Supporters were optimistic that their team of '91 could provide a similar result, although at this stage of the competition matches were played over two legs. Tottenham, one of England's biggest and most famous clubs, included Paul Stewart, Paul Allen, Gordon Durie and Gary Lineker – although the England striker was out injured for this game, which gave Roger a little relief from the pressure.

A nearly full house of 11,500 at the Vetch Field saw the home team run out 1-0 winners thanks to a goal from striker Jimmy Gilligan. Roger was in fine form and able to stop anything that Tottenham threw at him, the First Division side being constantly thwarted as they piled on the pressure looking for the equaliser. Such was Roger's performance that night, the competition sponsors, Rumbelows, named him as their man of the match and awarded him with the prize of a colour television after the game. For many years, this took pride of place in the corner of the Freestone living room and served as a memento of his Swansea debut proper. Even now, the set is still in the family, with Roger's in-laws making use of it.

Further praised was heaped on Roger by the Tottenham manager Peter Shreeves, who cited him as the main factor in Swansea's win. Frank Burrows commented that although it was a great game, he was more concerned with the League fixture against Peterborough the following Saturday, an encounter which Swansea won 1-0, Roger again being named man of the match to continue his home-coming fairytale. Another man of the match award came in the next game against Shrewsbury at Gay Meadow, and it was evident that Frank Burrows' faith in Roger as a top-class 'keeper was justified and Swansea had a special player on their books.

Swansea travelled to White Hart Lane for the second leg to try and defend their lead. Unfortunately, Tottenham had bought Gary Lineker back into the side, and his hat-trick helped the home team to a resounding 5-1 win on the night, Spurs winning a place in the next round with a 5-2 aggregate score. Even though it was a heavy defeat, Roger held happy memories of the tie and knew that he was going to be happy at Swansea, whose supporters had quickly taken to him. That night over a thousand Swans fans praised their new 'keeper at White Hart Lane, unaware that he would remain their heroic number one for many years to come.

Roger could not take part in the Cup Winners Cup tie against Monaco. Registration rules for UEFA competitions meant that players had to be registered early and Roger had missed the deadline. He took his place in the stand to watch the home leg, the Swans going down 2-1, Andy Legg scoring their goal. He was then left at home in Wales as the rest of the squad travelled to the Principality of Monaco to take part in the second leg. Maybe it was a blessing in disguise, as they equalled their heaviest defeat in top competition, going down 8-0 to plummet out of European competition with a 10-1 aggregate score.

Roger was confirmed as the first choice 'keeper at The Vetch when further man of the match awards followed against Merthyr in the Welsh Cup and Stoke City in a home League game, both performances helping secure victories for Swansea as they continued their good form and pulled away from the bottom end of the table. Frank Burrows was a manager that Roger could get on with and relate to. Although not one to mince his words, Frank was a fair man and someone that the players respected, although Roger was aware that if he said something then it was remembered for a long time. In his own words, 'Frank was a bit wild at times, and rumours that he threw a few things about are true. He would throw anything he could get his hands on if he was angry – put it this way you listened to him when he had something to say, if you didn't you were in trouble, big trouble. But he didn't rule us with an iron fist, he was an angry man at times, but also clever in his tactics and just wanted us to play good football. He was as good a manager as you could wish to have, he was approachable and understanding too. He had a lot of knowledge on the game, and managers like Harry Redknapp respected him – which showed when we had the likes of Frank Lampard junior at Swansea on loan. Frank Lampard arrived in his old car having been told to go to Swansea by Harry and get in the team, I don't think Frank even knew where Swansea was before he looked at it on the map. But he was a class player at seventeen, head and shoulders above players of the same age and probably better than a lot of players we had at Swansea at the time.'

Morale was high at Swansea when Burrows was there and the players enjoyed a good team spirit. This was demonstrated in the strange competition that the players used to run between themselves. The Swansea Biscuit Challenge involved eating ten dry biscuits in the shortest time possible. Anyone that has tried something similar will be aware that your mouth gets parched very quickly, and one of the rules of the competition was that drinks were not allowed. It was a case of stamina and the ability to eat – both things that Roger classed himself as an expert on. The races usually came down to a straight fight between Roger and Mark Harris, one of the central defenders that marshalled the Swansea defence at the time. Nicknamed 'Chopper' after the famous Chelsea defender of the 1970s, Harris had come a long way since he made his debut in a 1-6 home reverse to Reading. Now established as one of the crowd's favourites on the field, he also had an appetite that could match Roger's. Many a biscuit competition came down to a tussle between the two of them, but almost inevitably Roger came out on top to take the title. He had a big appetite and maybe didn't eat things that professional sportsmen should, but he enjoyed his food.

It was a comment from Frank Burrows that made Roger think he should change his eating habits. Frank declared that Roger was a good footballer and that could go a long way in the game – but he needed to lose some weight and get his diet and attitude to food right. This made Roger decide that he needed to diet there and then and make sure that his weight did not become a problem or a hindrance to his career. Although probably eating a similar amount of food after going on the diet, it was now the right kind of food and Roger will always remain grateful to Frank for his comment, although at the time it may have seemed a bit harsh. It was indeed a time to knuckle down and heed all pieces of advice that he could. Learning from people with greater experience could only help his career, and Bobby Smith was another person that Roger grew to respect as a coach and learned a lot from. Like Burrows, Bobby knew the game and took no nonsense. Roger liked the fact that you knew where you stood with him and respected his viewpoint, even if he did not always agree with it.

Jimmy Rimmer was also working part-time at The Vetch. Jimmy had been a European Cup winner with Aston Villa and had also played for Manchester United. Now settled in Swansea after his years at the club, he helped out with the coaching at The Vetch, as well as running his own golfing shop in the city centre. Unlike Frank and Bobby, Roger did not agree with the Jimmy's methods. Very much of the old school coaching approach, Jimmy passionately believed that you worked yourself as hard as you possibly could in order to become a better player. Roger remembers many times at The Vetch when the only time he would relent and let you rest was when you were about to be physically sick – Roger vividly remembers crouching on his hands and knees on the pitch with a ball being thrown for him to dive at before getting back up to do it all over again. Often these sessions left Roger feeling mentally and physically drained: surely not the best preparation for any sportsman preparing for a match? Jimmy's methods were certainly not appreciated by Roger and he believes that had the trainer stayed at the club then his own ability as a goalkeeper would not have progressed as much as it has. Roger believes that you have to work hard to further your career as a professional – but not to the point where you really didn't enjoy it and felt like throwing up.

When Roger joined the Swans in 1991/92, they were engaged in another campaign of mid-table safety. Never pushing for promotion or the play-offs, or being threatened by relegation, Swansea were spending their fourth season in the division and were widely known as one of the better mid-table sides. Roger spent the season establishing himself firmly as the first-choice goalkeeper, becoming part of a long tradition of solid Swansea stoppers and earning the appreciation of the fans.

Ten years earlier, Swansea City had been playing football at the summit of English football. It was a rise from bottom to top that they achieved in four years – and one that eventually almost sent the club out of existence. Swansea had survived for two years in the top flight, finishing sixth in their first season. During that time, the top sides of the generation (Manchester United, Liverpool, Tottenham, Arsenal and Ipswich) were all beaten with apparent ease by the Swans. However, financial problems had seen them drop back down to the bottom division and even, for a few hours in 1985, go out of existence.

The supporters longed for the better days again, but accepted that the rise would perhaps need to be slower and steadier this time around. When Roger arrived, they were beginning to believe that the club could seriously challenge for a return to the higher divisions. With 1992/93 seeing the foundation of the Premiership and the escalation of big-money television coverage of the game, promotion was becoming more and more important. With this in mind, Swansea City mounted a strong campaign for promotion. Towards the end of 1991/92, the club had ventured into the transfer market, John Cornforth, a playmaking midfielder, joining from Sunderland (he was to be a team-mate of Roger's at international level as well as club level in years to come). Also arriving at the club, during the close season, was Colin West, a one-time Rangers player. Hopes were high that this could be the year for promotion.

Colin had competed at the highest level – although at times he let everyone know it. Roger remembers one occasion against Merthyr in the Welsh Cup. This fixture had almost become an annual occurrence, the two sides seemingly always being drawn against each other at some stage. Although Swansea were a Football League club and Merthyr only semi-professional, such distinctions seemed to count for very little as the two sides regularly exchanged defeats. In this particular year, the game was played at Pennydarren Park – and it was a game that maybe Colin seemed to believe was beneath him. Merthyr had an ex-Swansea player, Terry Boyle, in their defence who Roger knew well from his loan spell. Boyle was someone that you did not mess with. Having previously played for both Cardiff and Swansea, he had a reputation throughout South Wales as a hard man to be underestimated only at your peril. Colin was to learn this the difficult way. Some of the pre-game talk in the dressing room was of Boyle, and those that had played with him gave their warnings of what to expect when they got out on the pitch. Colin, with a lot of self-belief and maybe a little arrogance, commented 'Who is this Terry Boyle anyway?' Swansea lost the game 2-0 and Boyle had Colin in his pocket throughout. Never getting a sniff at goal during the game, Merthyr were the better side and, were it not for Roger, the Swans would have gone down by a larger margin to their underdog opponents. In the dressing room after the game, Frank Burrows had a face like thunder, although his wrath was saved mainly for Colin, Burrows looking the hapless player straight in the eye and saying 'You asked who Terry Boyle was, well now you fucking know exactly who he is!'

During Roger's first full campaign there was another cause for celebration. The Freestone's second child, Lauren Michelle, was born on 10 December 1992 at the Royal Gwent hospital, weighing in at 7lb 10oz. Roger phoned his father soon after Lauren's birth. Having four grandsons already, Eddie was so shocked to hear that he had a granddaughter that he dropped the phone. Roger's family was complete.

Swansea's League form was reasonable in 1992/93 and they hovered on the edge of the play-offs. They also enjoyed an eventful run in the FA Cup. All lower division sides entered the cup at the first round stage and, with that initial hurdle successfully negotiated, Swansea drew Exeter City away in the second round. As with the match against Merthyr, this was a renewal of old acquaintances, Exeter providing the opposition for several Swansea cup ties during recent years.

Swansea did not let their travelling support down on their trip to the West Country. Comfortably winning with less than ten minutes to go at St James Park on a dark December Saturday afternoon, the floodlights failed and the referee led the players off the field. Talk in the Swansea dressing room was that of a 'fix' as they wondered if this was more than a co-incidence. The referee called into both dressing rooms to advise that he was giving the situation another half an hour before abandoning the game. Swansea were understandably disappointed with this, believing that there was no way that Exeter would have got back into the game and feeling that they should have been awarded the victory. Frank Burrows was in typical form, turning the air blue with a string of expletives. When the lights did not come back on, the referee duly abandoned the match and the replay was ordered.

Unlike recent times, FA Cup replays were scheduled for the following midweek and, three days after darkness fell on St James Park, Exeter and Swansea again lined up to do battle. Fortunately, justice was done as Swansea ran out 5-2 victors and entered the third round of the FA Cup, going into the draw with some of the biggest names in the domestic game. The third round was to prove just as eventful as the second, but initially for reasons other than the game itself, which was to be against Oxford United at the Vetch. The home draw had given the team chance to progress further in the competition, but football was the last thing on Roger's mind as the morning of the match dawned.

Sue had been suffering from a bout of tonsillitis during the week leading up to the Oxford game. Roger followed his usual routine in the build-up to the match, having no idea of the turn of events just around the corner. Sue was rushed into hospital on the Saturday morning, after finding it increasingly difficult to breathe. Roger was overcome with panic and he completely forgot about the upcoming cup tie. Sue was diagnosed with a case of quinsy, an inflammation of the tonsils caused by an abscess. Fortunately, the hospital were able to reduce the inflammation with some antibiotics and her breathing gradually returned to normal. Amazingly, on Sue's insistence, Roger was told to travel to Swansea to take part in the Oxford game.

Few supporters who entered the Vetch that day would have realised just what their goalkeeper had been through hours earlier, and it was to Roger's credit that he was able to keep a clean sheet as Swansea drew 0-0 to force a replay at the Manor Ground. These ties with Oxford brought Roger face to face with a player who was to become a team-mate in years to come, United's Nick Cusack literally making his mark on Roger in the replay. During the game, both men went to challenge for a high ball in the penalty area and Nick caught Roger with his elbow, cutting him in the process. It was, however, Roger who was to have the last laugh, as the match headed from extra-time into penalties with the teams locked at 2-2. After the sides had exchanged four successful spot-kicks each, Roger pulled off a fine penalty save from Chris Allen, leaving Keith Walker to score the winning penalty and send Swansea into the fourth round of the FA Cup.

The FA Cup run was to end in the fourth round against Grimsby, who were in Division One and enjoying a fine run of form in the League. The original game at the Vetch ended in a draw and, maybe appropriately for this particular cup run, City made the long journey for a replay the following Tuesday evening. On a cold night in the North East, they were beaten 2-0, Roger being unable to stop one shot that flew into the top corner of the net.

Thankfully, Swansea's League form was still good, and as the season drew to a close they found themselves just outside the play-off positions. West Bromwich Albion were pushing hard for automatic promotion, and Swansea travelled there knowing that both sides needed the points. The Baggies were by far the better team on the day, and were 2-0 up with just 15 minutes to go. Frank Burrows seemed powerless to do anything as his play-off ambitions appeared to be taking a backward step, but he introduced Steve Thornber for Alan Davies in a desperate attempt to salvage something from the game. There was no way that Frank could have envisaged quite what was going to happen next, as Steve

Thornber scored three goals in an amazing ten-minute spell for the Welsh side. On the back of that unlikely win, Swansea eventually finished fifth in the table – to face West Brom in their play-off semi-final.

Unfortunately, a few days after that remarkable 3-2 result at The Hawthorns, Alan Davies, a one-time Manchester United player, FA Cup winner and Welsh international, took his own life in a remote area of Swansea. This was a tragic loss of a great talent.

The first leg of the play-offs was scheduled for the Sunday after Cup Final day, and was to be played at the Vetch Field. As the day dawned, heavy rain was falling over Swansea and Frank prepared his side for what he knew was going to be a very tough battle. Despite the downpour, Swansea fans turned up en masse and a full Vetch Field had an electric atmosphere. Swansea were 2-0 up and seemingly on their way to a comfortable first leg win when the visitors won a corner.

Roger positioned Andy Macfarlane on the line. The corner was taken and the ball sent into the box, where it hit Macfarlane on the head before bouncing onto his knee and into the goal – a lifeline for West Brom. A few choice words were exchanged between the goalkeeper and his defender (whose customary role was as a striker), Roger's argument revolving around why the ball was not cleared. The own goal gave West Brom a life-line for the second leg, which was to take place just three days later at The Hawthorns. The winners of the tie would be heading to Wembley for a one-off shot at Division One football the following season.

Although Roger had played at the highest level, he was not prepared for the atmosphere that was to greet him and his Swansea team-mates during the second game. It was an experience that will live with him for ever. A capacity crowd of 28,000 supporters were crammed into the ground that night, with the West Brom fans deploying an unusual chant that involved jumping up and down singing 'Boing Boing Baggies'. Whilst this might not sound particularly intimidating, more than 20,000 people doing it was a strangely oppressive sight. Crushed into a corner of the ground, 3,500 Swans fans did their best to encourage their team.

Swansea knew that they would have to survive some early pressure if they were to get through to the final. Sadly, not only did they fail to keep the lead beyond the opening ten minutes, but they conceded two goals during that period and found themselves behind on aggregate. This only served to swell the noise coming from the home fans and, although the travelling Welsh support tried their best, they could not match the volume of the massed West Brom supporters.

Swansea were thrown a lifeline when West Brom were reduced to ten men. They had been gradually getting themselves back into the game following the early setbacks and with the advantage of an extra player it started to look as though they could pull back the deficit. As the Swans piled on the pressure, a solid penalty appeal was turned down – Roger still maintains that the referee bottled out in the face of the intimidating noise coming from the home fans – and Frank decided to send on substitute Colin West to try and get the goal his team desperately needed. Colin was to have an impact on the game, but not in the way that Swansea fans would have hoped.

Within two minutes of being sent onto the pitch, Colin was heading the other way. He had stamped on an opposing player and, quite rightly, the referee had brandished a red card. Swansea's chance of victory left the pitch with Colin, and West Brom hung on to their lead to claim a place in the play-off final. Once again, Frank had a few words choice words to say to Colin. He was livid that one of his senior professionals had acted in such a way to cost them the game. Swansea were playing the better football at the time of the incident, Frank and the rest of the team being confident that if they had managed to take the game into extra time that they would have gone on and won it. Colin's refusal to apologise to his Swansea team-mates added to the despondent atmosphere in the dressing room. Swansea had, in effect, lost a two-goal lead from just before half time in the first game to lose 3-2, and there was little anyone could say to provide consolation.

Roger was confident that if his side had managed to keep a clean sheet at home they would have won the tie. As it was, they now had to face another season in Division Two. Roger is philosophical about the 1992/93 play-off semi-final disappointment: 'I agree to some extent that Colin didn't do us any favours by doing what he did, but it was a charged atmosphere and, to be honest, Leggy could have turned the game for us had he taken his chances. So, even though Colin lost his head and got sent off are you telling me that he was the reason why we were going to win the game? Because if you are then why did Frank not start him? Okay, it's better to have eleven players on the pitch, and Colin's actions didn't go down too well in the dressing room, but he was not the only reason we lost the game and went out of the play-offs. There was more to it than that, and when you come up against teams like West Brom you realise that they are going to be tougher than anything else you had come up against that season. They were better than us all round, and they beat us, and Colin West was not the reason why we lost. That was down to all of us, and the fact that we didn't strengthen the squad when we should have done – fine in hindsight I know, but true.'

If Swansea had won that game and gone on to win promotion they would have missed out on the glory that was to follow the very next season, but at the time it was a disappointed Roger and Swansea City that went into the summer break reflecting on what might have been. Few people would have realised, as the players reported back for pre-season training, that Swansea City was less than eight months away from one of its greatest days – a Wembley trip on a Sunday afternoon in April to play in front of 50,000 fans.

The nearly squad. From left to right, back row: Tony Cullen, Reuben Agboola, Colin Pascoe, Des Lyttle, Russell Coughlin. Middle row: Steve Jenkins, John Ford, Andy McFarlane, Steve Mcmahon, Mark Harris, Colin West, Keith Walker. Front row: Paul Wimbleton, Shaun Chapple, Roger Freestone, John Cornforth, James Heeps, Jason Bowen, Andy Legg.

Roger, Des Lyttle and Andy Legg pose with Cameron Robb, the team mascot on 8 May 1983.

6

WEMBLEY GLORY WITH THE SWANS

The League form of the 1993/94 season was not as consistent as in the previous campaign, and Swansea maintained a respectable mid-table position. Frank Burrows was, however, assembling a side that performed on the big occasions, with some memorable performances that had the local support buzzing in cup competitions. The team, which had taken him eighteen months to assemble, included youth players in Andrew Legg, Jason Bowen and Steve Jenkins and some typically astute Burrows purchases in Kwame Ampadu, John Cornforth, Mark Clode and Andy Cook. The attack was led by two tall, lanky centre forwards, Andy Macfarlane and Steve Torpey (a purchase from Bradford City), and the defence was shored up by one the best 'keepers in the lower divisions, Roger Freestone. Burrows himself was a chairman's dream. A man with a reputation for toughness, he was passionate, committed and aggressive, running the team strongly but fairly. He was also a man who would spend hours covering the length and breadth of the country on the lookout for new players – the signings of John Ford, Des Lyttle and John Williams, who between them netted the club almost £1 million in transfer fees when they were eventually sold – providing a testimony to his dedication and discernment.

As with most cup runs, the road to eventual glory in the Autoglass Trophy began in the strangest of places. In this particular instance, Roger joined his Swansea City team-mates as they headed to the South West of England for a tie against Plymouth at Home Park – a ground which at the time was similar to The Vetch in that it was in need of development and had seen better days. That night, in driving rain, Swansea celebrated a hard-fought 3-1 victory, thanks largely to a very impressive performance from Darren Perrett. The team had taken the first steps on the road to Wembley but, as is almost always the case in this competition, interest in the early rounds was minimal – this being reflected in the fact that Swansea's travelling support that night numbered a meagre 62.

Although Swansea won the game comfortably, Frank Burrows recognised the need for more aggression in his midfield and signed Chris Burns on loan from his old club, Portsmouth. Burns fitted the bill for what Frank saw was missing. Burns, to this day, remembers his time in a Swansea shirt with great affection tinged with extreme disappointment. He recognised Frank Burrows' passion and commitment to the cause and held him in high regard. The respect that Burns had for Burrows as a manager was greater than that he had for any other he had played under. He believed that Frank's passion for the game rubbed off on everybody at the club, a major factor in the 1993/94 side's success.

Sadly for Welsh football in general, passions off the pitch were sometimes directed in a totally unacceptable way. A midweek evening fixture in December saw a South Wales derby match that is now infamous amongst supporters of both Cardiff and Swansea. The game was scheduled to finish at 9.30p.m., but events dictated that it was to conclude almost an hour late as Swansea and Cardiff fans fought on the pitch and stands throughout the night – which led to a ban on away supporters at the fixture for a number of years. This is something that did and still does concern Roger greatly. The uncontrolled rivalry between Swansea and Cardiff dismays the man from Newport. Although he appreciates and recognises that both clubs inspire very passionate support, he does not understand the need for constant battling with each other – a problem that has blighted both clubs for a considerable period of time.

Back in the Autoglass Trophy, Exeter City were beaten 2-1 at The Vetch after extra time in the second round. The Swans fans were starting to think about Wembley. The third round (or Southern quarter-final) opponents were Port Vale, the current holders of the trophy. With more people now taking an interest in the competition, Swansea were again dominant and defeated the Potteries side 1-0, Chris Burns netting the winner from 25 yards. The mood in the dressing room was now one of expectation – Wembley was there for the taking and the only thing that remained was the drawing of the balls to see against who and where the next match would take place.

It was to be a tough away tie for the Southern Area semi-final, Leyton Orient at Brisbane Road. Having often been unsuccessful at this ground in the past, there was a lot of anxiety amongst the increased away support of 500. The side had been bolstered with another loan signing, Matthew Rush, secured through Burrow's strong connections with his club, West Ham. Rush was a young exciting midfield player with a thorough Hammers pedigree. With his influence playing a vital part, Swansea cast aside previous history at Brisbane Road to win comfortably with goals from Steve Torpey and Shaun Chapple.

Swansea City were now just a couple of games from Wembley, facing a two-legged Southern Area final against relative newcomers to the Football League, Wycombe Wanderers. If they were successful, Roger and his team-mates would be the first Welsh side to play at the famous old stadium since 1927.

The first leg of the tie was to be played at the Vetch Field and Swansea's supporters turned up in their thousands to get behind the team. Wycombe were swept aside with a well-deserved 3-1 victory, two goals from Colin Pascoe and one from Jason Bowen sending the Vetch crowd wild with delight. Bowen was being watched by Newcastle United at the time, and had just returned from a week's trial at St James Park. Manchester United were also keen on the player, along with Sheffield United and Leeds. Roger had very little to do that evening, and such was the nature of Swansea's performance that the tie could, and maybe should, have been all over once the referee blew his whistle for the end of the match. After the game, Frank Burrows stated that The Swans should have won by four or five goals. He went on to say that he was approaching the highlight of his career, with Swansea City just one game from Wembley.

This was, however, not destined to be a smooth progression, and the players and supporters were in for an extremely tense night at Wycombe's Adams Park. To lighten the mood before the game, Doug Sharpe, the Swansea chairman, caused a great deal of fun amongst the players when he was pictured in the Welsh Press wearing a miner's hat that had not seen the light of day since 1964, when Swansea had played at Villa Park in an FA Cup semi-final against Preston. It was also at this stage of the competition that the Home Secretary, Michael Howard MP, declared himself a Swansea fan, although the travelling 62 at Plymouth a few months before would have laughed at this newfound affinity. As far as Roger was concerned, the side deserved it for all their hard work under the guidance of Frank Burrows, the club's most successful manager since John Toshack. All the team had to do now was finish the job that they had started at Home Park. Roger was desperate to repay the faith that Swansea had shown in him and reward the support of the fans with an appearance at the most famous stadium in the world. Swansea was now part of Roger's adopted family, and he was proud to describe himself as a 'Swansea Jack'. Although his time at Chelsea had been enjoyable in parts and Newport would always hold a place in his heart, his love for his present club was without doubt the real thing.

Frank Burrows prepared his side for the game, aware that his two loan stars, Chris Burns and Matthew Rush, would be back with their clubs by the time the final was played. It was with great excitement that the travelling North Bank headed East to Adams Park for the return leg, 3,000 of them turning one area of Adams Park into a mini Vetch Field for the night. The knowledge of what the team would achieve with the right result sent Roger's nerves jangling. As the teams took the field, Roger was amazed at the volume and intensity of the Welsh National Anthem emanating from the Swansea supporters. He also remembers hearing the first rendition of what was to become a regular feature of Swansea games, 'Falling In Love With You'.

Frank Burrows had warned his team that Wycombe would not sit back and so it proved, Wycombe taking the game by the scruff of the neck and soon scoring. The tension mounted as the home team continued to pile the pressure on the Swansea goal. Roger sent several glances across to the bench, the sight of Frank Burrows suffering every possible emotion giving him even more determination to succeed for the sake of the man who had given him this new lease of life in bringing him back to Wales. With its owner under tremendous pressure, Burrows' trademark flat cap was being waved all over the place. Roger was painfully aware that a second goal past him would send the tie into extra time and effectively put Wycombe ahead on the away goals rule.

The last few minutes of the match seemed to last forever and are etched in Roger's memory: 'Wycombe had a corner and it was clear to me that all the players were nervous and this was shown in the way that we played and defended. The corner came across and I managed to catch it. It was so close to the end of the game and as I caught it and kicked it upfield I shanked the kick about forty yards. It went straight to one of their players and they started their next attack. The referee had now played so much injury time that we almost thought we were in extra time, and were desperately hanging on to our slim advantage.' A massive roar erupted as the referee bought the game to an end and Roger sprinted towards the dressing room as the Swansea support invaded the pitch to celebrate the aggregate victory. Frank Burrows took his side back out onto the pitch after ten minutes and Roger celebrated with the fans, revelling in the culmination of an ambition which had begun on the streets of Rogerstone many years earlier.

In the dressing room after the game, a friend of Matthew Rush ordered forty-four bottles of Budweiser with his compliments. The players enjoyed the beer and raised a glass to Matthew's absent friend for his generosity – although a couple of weeks later the full story regarding the 'free' drinks emerged when the club received an invoice for the bottles and a cheque had to be sent to Wycombe to cover the cost. This was, however, a small price to pay for what would be one of the biggest paydays in the club's history.

Between the Wycombe game and the Wembley match, against Huddersfield Town, there were vital League points to play for. Although Roger carried on with his normal professionalism, thoughts of Wembley were never far from his mind. Indeed, the famous old stadium was in the thoughts of most Swansea fans and, as the club survived on crowds of 4,000-5,000, they found themselves selling 20,000 tickets for the Autoglass Trophy final, as the population of the city prepared to turn all routes from Wales to Wembley into a sea of black and white.

The players were also busy in preparation for the biggest day of most of their careers. Roger, along with the rest of the team, was fitted for the obligatory cup final suit as press calls, a cup final strip and talk of Swansea glory at Wembley detracted from the League programme.

The final was scheduled for Sunday 24 April 1994, and the team made their way to the Vetch Field the previous day as the majority of British clubs prepared for their League games that afternoon. Previous results between the sides in the current season have given the Swans a 1-0 victory at The Vetch and a 1-1 draw at Leeds Road.

Roger and Richard Jones (who went on to manage Barry Town) travelled back to Newport to meet the team coach at the Country Court Hotel. Roger, being Roger, decided that he would visit his favourite chip shop near his old stamping ground at Somerton Park and the two of them indulged in a bag each. The squad and management then travelled directly to Wembley to take a look at the famous old stadium. They indulged in an acclimatising walk on the pitch, looked round the changing rooms and walked up the Wembley steps – each of them hoping that they would be making the same trip the next day as Autoglass Trophy winners.

To Roger, an empty Wembley Stadium was an awesome sight and his first experience of the ground was one that will live with him forever. He tried to imagine the sight of it the next day, as 50,000 Swansea and Huddersfield fans would turn it into what was described at the time as an 'England *v*. Wales' event. Roger joined the rest of the players as they headed to the overnight hotel for dinner. After finishing an enjoyable team meal they headed to their rooms at 7.30 p.m. – under the instruction of the management that it was straight to bed, in preparation for the big day ahead.

As one of the jokers in the Swansea pack, Roger decided that, despite Frank Burrows' strict pre-match regime, it was time to give Ken Davies, the team coach driver, some serious stick and devised his own little campaign, enlisting the help of midfield general John Cornforth. Ken was in his seventies and had driven the team bus for several years. Roger and Corny presented him with a team tracksuit, which Ken received gleefully, touched that he was being honoured in this way. However, the downside of this gift for Ken was that Roger and John now had the key for his room. The first item in their plan of attack was to remove all the screws from the legs of Ken's bed, so that it would collapse when he sat on it. Roger and Corny were now in full flow, and decided that the next thing on their list was to add cling film to the toilet seat.

Roger's grin is very wide as he recalls the escapades of that night. This is one of the happiest memories of his career and shows why he is one of the most popular players of his generation. Ken was always one to have a pint or two before he retired for the night and he headed off to his room around 11.00 p.m. His first point of call when he got to the room, as anyone who has taken on board a few drinks, was the toilet. Not in the clearest frame of mind, Ken unleashed the contents of his bladder and was immediately the victim of the Freestone Cornforth Power Shower. Ken was always to become the focus for Roger's pranks. A few years later he had a sandwich complete with Roger's false teeth which he retrieved from his own mouth whilst driving the team to Norwich for a League cup game.

Despite the large possible list of suspects – Swansea City had a travelling party of forty-four players and staff – Ken knew who the culprit was and immediately yelled 'You bastard, Freestone'. As Swansea fans up and down the country struggled to sleep ahead of their club's biggest day, Roger was sniggering under his bedclothes at a mental picture of Ken, some cling film and a Swansea christening to be proud of. Ken left the bathroom to recover from this unexpected surprise and decided to rest while plotting any possible revenge. All thoughts of retribution promptly left his mind, however, as the bed collapsed under his weight.

The following morning all talk was of the unfortunate events that had befallen the hapless Ken. Roger and John's pranks were enjoyed by the entire party – with the possible exception of Ken himself – and helped take the pressure off what was a harrowing morning for all of them. This was indicative of the great team spirit that the players enjoyed. It is to Frank Burrow's credit that he recognised this and did not direct any harsh words towards two of his senior professionals, despite their breaking of his curfew the night before.

For their breakfast on the big day, most players ordered carbohydrate-laden toast and cereal. Roger, however, fitted as much bacon, eggs, sausage and tomato as he could on his plate. He has never taken any real criticism regarding his dislike for the traditional pre-match meal, and Burrows always let him enjoy a fry up, safe in the knowledge that he would not eat anything else before the game.

As the Wembley experience drew nearer, the players were allowed to go for a walk around eleven o'clock, either individually or in groups, to contemplate what they would be facing that afternoon. Despite not actually eating anything, Roger sat down with the rest of the team at twelve o'clock. Alongside him was Mark Harris, who probably considered himself the luckiest player at Wembley that day. Had it not have been for a West Wales Senior Cup game rearranged with Haverfordwest County, Mark Harris would not have played in the final. Fortunately for him, the FA had allowed the game to count as an official fixture to set off against his domestic suspension. Frank Burrows named his Swansea team for the big match and the chosen squad set off to make both Swansea and Welsh footballing history.

At 12.15, the players boarded the coach and Ken, fresh from a shower of the proper kind, drove them to the stadium. As the coach arrived at Wembley that day, Roger was astounded at the sight of Wembley Way covered in a mass of black, blue and white as both sets of supporters converged on the Twin Towers. To Roger, this summed up the day. After scanning the crowd for familiar faces, often seen in far less glamorous surroundings, the team made their way into the ground. The proud look on Frank Burrows' face as the team prepared in the dressing rooms prior to the game formed another of Roger's best memories of the day. This was a moment that Frank had worked hard for, and the culmination of several years of planning. This was his team at the home of football.

Roger again made his mark in this game. As early as the seventh minute, Swansea were awarded a free kick just outside their own penalty area, which Roger took. The ball flew half the length of the Wembley pitch and landed at the feet of Andy Macfarlane, who drove it past the outstretched hand of Steve Francis in the Huddersfield goal to put the Swans 1-0 up and send thousands of Welsh fans behind the Freestone goal delirious with joy. Ironically, Roger had replaced Steve Francis at Chelsea seven years earlier.

The two teams exchanged chances for the remainder of the game and, despite some resolute defending, Swansea and Roger were unable to prevent the equaliser and the game headed into extra time. Both sides had chances to finish the match, Jason Bowen hitting the Huddersfield bar with a shot that Roger, watching from the other end, was convinced was going in. It was, therefore a matter of ten penalties and the possibility of sudden death. Roger knew that this was his chance to become a hero and write his name all over the history books of Swansea City and the back pages of the Welsh football press. He was also aware that his performance in the course of the shoot-out could make him responsible for his team's failure.

Thankfully for Roger and every Swansea fan, it was as a hero that he left the stadium that afternoon. With Swansea ahead on penalties, Huddersfield had to score to keep themselves in the contest. Roger guessed correctly, made the save, and one end of Wembley erupted. Roger admits that he had been concentrating so hard on trying to stop the penalties he faced that he did not realise it was the winning save until he was mobbed by his jubilant team-mates. Swansea City had won the Autoglass Trophy.

The City of Swansea celebrated that weekend with massive press exposure, as the rugby team had also won the Welsh Championship to make it the most successful sporting weekend in the city's history. Indeed, Cardiff Devils' achievement in reaching a Wembley ice hockey final the same day was hardly mentioned, such was the adulation heaped on Roger and his Swansea team-mates. No-one was more proud than the goalkeeper from Rogerstone as the players picked up a chairman's bonus of £2,500. Of course, the prize itself had to be presented to the winning team, Roger taking his place second in line behind captain John Cornforth to lift the Autoglass Trophy at Wembley. He will never forget the moment when it was passed to him and he turned to show it to the travelling Jack Army. Naturally, the players celebrated with a few beers before boarding the coach to head back to Swansea and reality, an important League fixture against Port Vale on the agenda just two days later.

Frank Burrows had achieved something that no other Swansea manager had, although over the next season Roger and his Swansea team-mates would try and outdo the class of 1994.

John Cornforth and Roger having just won the cup at Wembley. The ghosts of 1927 have finally been laid to rest.

The 1994 Autoglass winning squad. From left to right, back row: Jon Brady, Dave Barnhouse, Martin Hayes, Shaun Chapple, Andy Cook. Middle row: Keith Walker, John Ford, Mark Harris, Roger Freestone, Steve Torpey, Andy Macfarlane, Richard Jones. Front row: Mark Clode, Steve Jenkins, John Hodge, John Cornforth, Jason Bowen, Colin Pascoe, Jonathan Coates.

7

THE YEAR OF THE CUP RUN

As the summer drew on, Swansea returned to pre-season training with a shiny Autoglass Trophy sitting proudly at the forefront of the Vetch trophy cabinet. Roger was entering his fourth season at the club. Frank Burrows had transformed his career and, with Sue and the children also very happy, Roger had every reason to feel contented and optimistic.

The previous season had been special for him, but this one was to bring rewards of a different sort. Recognition of the way that Swansea were playing came in the form of a Welsh call-up for Roger, along with John Cornforth and Steve Jenkins. Cornforth was widely regarded as one of the most accomplished midfield players outside the top flight, whilst Steve Jenkins was a right-back who gave everything to the cause, and was respected by colleagues and opponents alike. For Roger, international recognition capped a remarkable turnaround in fortunes – four years earlier he had been contemplating a life outside football.

The FA Cup had bought some memorable days in Swansea's history and no doubt will bring many more in the future. The competition was always something that the players enjoyed as a distraction from League games and, as any fan of a lower division or non-League club will tell you, the prospect of playing for one of the top clubs in England is on everyone's mind when first round day arrives.

Six years earlier, Swansea had travelled to Anfield for a third round replay. Roger had been at the club during the build-up up to the match and realised what a big draw meant to the supporters. Furthermore, because he had been denied the opportunity to play in the Liverpool tie, the ambition of performing for the club in a similar situation was at the back of his mind as Swansea drew Walton & Hersham in the first round of the FA Cup.

Not many comparisons can be drawn between Walton & Hersham and Liverpool, but in the FA Cup everyone enters with a potential taste of glory. Swansea's big moments tend to come at places like Liverpool, while for non-League clubs, a 'cup final' can take place at a club like Swansea. Roger was aware that this was a tie that his team couldn't really win. You beat Walton & Hersham and everyone says that you were expected to do so; you lose and you can look forward to back page headlines about part-time postmen pulling off a cup upset.

However, there were to be no slip ups this time as Swansea beat Walton in the first round and then overcame Bashley in the second. As the third round draw was made, Roger thought of Chelsea, feeling that it would be nice to go to Stamford Bridge to play in the FA Cup. As much as he hadn't enjoyed his last couple of years there, he still held the place in his heart and would have loved a trip back there.

But a trip to Stamford Bridge was not on the cards for Roger and his Swansea team-mates as they were drawn against Middlesborough. The Teeside team were on a high at this time, under the leadership of ex-Manchester United captain Bryan Robson. The former England captain's first season was going well as Middlesborough were flying high at the top of the First Division and looking almost certain to return to the Premiership; they were also obvious favourites to progress in the FA Cup. The heavens over Swansea Bay opened on third round day, saturating the Vetch Field turf. Frank Burrows warned Roger and his team-mates what to expect with Middlesborough – Bryan Robson was a player who gave everything on the pitch, and his side were expected to do the same.

However, Swansea was a team bonding together well, and they knew that if they played at the top of their game they had a chance of getting an unexpected result. As it turned out, they did not let themselves down in front of a big home crowd as they secured a draw to take them to the North East for the replay. Despite trailing to a Middlesborough goal, a tremendous equaliser from John Ford stunning the First Division side and sending the home fans home happy.

Before the tie could be decided, the fourth round draw was made – Newcastle United or Blackburn Rovers *v.* Swansea City or Middlesborough. Frank Burrows was invited onto Sky Sports as a studio guest at the Newcastle *v.* Blackburn game, and all talk as Newcastle won was one of a North East derby. Roger remembers Frank returning from the studios, honoured that he had been given the chance to make his views known and aware that Swansea were now in the position that Walton & Hersham had been at the start of the run. They had nothing to lose. Everybody expected Middlesborough to win the game.

Doug Sharpe, the Swansea chairman, let the team travel into the North East on the Monday before the match. Roger knew what a cup run meant to a lower division club, both in terms of national media coverage and the cash generated from the games. Victory at The Riverside would mean a full house at Newcastle in the fourth round and a massive payday for Swansea City. Being underdogs was a good feeling for the players. They were able to relax and, although a few thoughts of St James Park were natural, they were focused on the task ahead. For Roger, of course, the replay bought back memories of his first taste of the big match atmosphere when he had played against Middlesborough with Newport, which was also the occasion of his first professional booking.

Swansea made an amazing start to the replay. Twenty minutes into the game, the Welsh side were 2-0 up thanks to a goal from Steve Torpey and a fine volley from David Penney. The Middlesborough players were stunned at the Swansea onslaught at the start of the game and couldn't recovered from the deficit, despite pulling one goal back. Swansea had carried off a major cup upset and 40,000 Geordie fans awaited them for a fourth round tie at St James' Park.

Frank was full of praise for his players after the game. Roger also fully appreciated the work of the team in front of him, none more so than Steve Torpey. Although the giant striker had suffered his share of criticism in the past, Roger admired the way he played the game and saw him as an important part of the team. Torpey commanded respect, amongst both team-mates and opponents, as a kind of 'governor' figure. This title was merely in fun as Torpey was from London, and Paul Ince was having a lot of stick at the time in the press.

Despite the distraction of the cup run, Swansea's League position was held and they were still in contention for a play-off place as they travelled to Newcastle. It was a massive day for Welsh football. Not only were Swansea embarking on this adventure, but Wrexham were travelling to Old Trafford for their own fourth round game. Neither side had been rated as having a chance and two easy home wins were expected for the Premiership sides. Besides the excitement of being in the FA Cup fourth round, the Newcastle game would also reunite Roger with an old acquaintance from his Newport days. Darren Peacock was a key player at the heart of the Magpies' defence, and Roger was looking forward to playing against him.

Newcastle were one of the most entertaining sides in England. Managed by Kevin Keegan, their style of football had made them many friends among neutrals. A full house at St James' Park is certainly something to behold, and as the teams took the field, Roger was amazed at the sea of black and white that welcomed him, as well as the passionate support coming from both sets of fans.

The game underway, Swansea almost got off to an incredible start. Martin Hayes, formerly of Arsenal and Celtic, broke clear with barely thirty seconds on the clock, and should have put Swansea a goal to the good. Roger always felt that Martin, like Colin West, was a very talented player who never fulfilled his potential at Swansea. Another first-half chance was missed when Steve Torpey saw his header saved at point blank range, and as the sides headed into the dressing room for the break, Swansea felt that they could easily have been a goal or two to the good. The second half was a different story, however, a Paul Kitson hat-trick sending Swansea home as 3-0 losers. The FA Cup run had come to an end, but Burrows' side had not disgraced themselves. For forty-five minutes they had worried one of the top sides in Europe. All that remained was for Roger and the rest of the Swansea side to thank the travelling fans for their enthusiastic support at the match. After the match, Roger was to receive an unusual accolade for his performance that day. As was becoming traditional, Frank Burrows allowed the side to have a portion of chips each after the game. When the food arrived, there was an extra serving for 'the goalkeeper that had played so well'. Roger had seen some unusual man of the match awards over the years, but this beat them all.

Despite defeat at St James' Park, Swansea's cup exploits that season were far from over. As defending champions, they were making a spirited defence of the Autoglass trophy. Wembley was beckoning again as they were drawn in the Southern Area semi-finals against Birmingham City at St Andrews. The game was to be one in which Swansea City would write their names in the history books of English football. Due to constant criticism of penalty shoot-outs to decide drawn games, the powers-that-be in World and European football were determined to find something new that could be deemed fairer and stop the farce of teams deliberately trying for penalties at the end of normal time. Golden Goals were on trial. No-one was sure that they would work, but with Euro '96 just one year away, the Autoglass Trophy got the system on trial. So far, the golden goal had not been needed, but the Birmingham *v*. Swansea tie duly went into extra time. Birmingham, a club which was almost certainly too big for the division they were playing in and were well on course to rectify that with promotion, were the competition favourites. It was a credit to both sides that they attacked and looked for the golden goal that would take them closer to a Wembley final. Swansea thought they had managed it when John Cornforth, the victorious captain the previous season, headed the ball against the Birmingham crossbar and watched it bounce down onto the goal line. In scenes reminiscent of the World Cup final of 1966, the Swansea players were convinced that they had scored and that the game was won.

Unfortunately for Roger and the lads, there was no Russian linesman on hand to award the goal and the game went on. The incident was to prove to be Swansea's only real chance of winning the game and it was Birmingham who took the step into the Southern Area final. Roger has been on the losing side in penalty shoot-outs and has conceded last-minute winners, but his feeling when the first golden goal in Britain went past him was one that he finds hard to describe. 'There is nothing that could prepare you for seeing a goal hit the net behind you and know that it's the end of the game. At least with last-minute goals or penalties you generally get another chance to try and fight back – but not this time.' It was maybe not the kind of record he wanted to set, but the new scheme was considered a success and later went onto be implemented in every major football competition. Since that St Andrews tie, golden goals decided the European Championship in 1996 and 2000, but it was Roger that felt the heartbreak first. Indeed, throughout his career, Roger has been less than orthodox in some of the things he does. Well-respected by most of the players in the lower divisions as a shot stopper, the 1995/96 season also saw him putting goals in at the other end.

Roger had seen very few goalkeepers scoring in his career, and had never managed to launch the ball from one end of the pitch to the other and catch his opposite number unawares or off his line. Swansea's regular penalty taker was John Cornforth. Usually fairly deadly from the spot, Cornforth had missed a few, and Frank Burrows decided to change the penalty taker. Colin Pascoe was handed the responsibility, but he missed as well and Frank was at his wits end with nobody wanting the job of trying to score from twelve yards. Roger could see that this worried his manager and felt that, as a goalkeeper, he could offer a different perspective, and asked Frank if he could take Swansea's next penalty. Frank agreed to the suggestion, and Roger spent some time in training sessions practising penalty kicks, in case the opportunity arose for him to take one.

That chance was to come at the Manor Ground in Oxford. A Swansea player was bundled over in the box and the referee pointed to the spot. Panic immediately overcame Roger. Was Frank serious? Should he just make the move to take the penalty? Roger looked over at the bench where his gaze was met by that of Burrows, who was waiting for him to move. Without further ado, Roger left his penalty area and jogged to the other end of the pitch, much to the amusement of the spectators.

Many thoughts entered Roger's head as he made his way towards the opposing penalty area. The most worrying of these was the question that, if he missed, did he have enough pace to get back before Oxford took the ball up the other end and scored a simple goal? Telling himself that this was not the time to be entertaining doubts – he had a job to do and just needed to make sure that he did it properly – he began his run-up to the ball. Roger connected well and looked up in time to see the net bulge. It flew into the top of the net, and Roger describes it as the best penalty he has ever seen! Roger Freestone had scored his first goal in professional football. As it turned out, it was also the winner and he had helped secure three valuable points for Swansea.

As he returned to the dressing room after the match, a strange feeling of panic hit him again. Although he had scored, his mind moved to what if he hadn't. He would now be walking into the dressing room to face the wrath of his manager. Other players may miss penalties, but at least they still have their goalkeeper behind them to back them up. Roger had seen Frank Burrows' displeasure close up and he did not really want incur it on himself.

Frank's temper at bad performances was something that all Swansea players knew about and feared – indeed, maybe his sides played such good football to avoid their manager's ferocious aspect. Roger remembers one Welsh Cup game at Rhyl where Frank's temper was brought to bear. At half time, the players entered the dressing room with the score still 0-0. The team thought this was alright, but Frank had a different opinion. The reaction that greeted them from the manager was a bit of a shock to most players, but a big shock to a select few. Darren Perrett was first target for Frank's rage as a punch told him what his performance had been like. Moments later, Steve Jenkins was subjected to a flying jar of Vaseline as Frank left his players aware that he was not best pleased with their showing thus far in the game. Frank further vented his anger on the football skip, but unluckily for him, the skip was not taking it as meekly as some of the players and all but broke Frank's foot in half. The sight of an incredibly angry manager hobbling round the dressing room in agony made hard work for the joker inside Roger as he tried his best to stifle a laugh. Full-on displays of temper like this from Frank were rare, however, and Roger freely admits that when they were on the receiving end they usually deserved it.

That trip to Rhyl was also good fun for other reasons. The team travelled up on the Friday for the Saturday game and stayed at Llandudno. As they pulled into the North Wales town on a glorious day, the team started collecting a kitty on the bus. This was not for anyone in particular, but would be awarded to the first person who dared to jump into the sea and swim out. As there was money involved, Mr Freestone was at the front of the queue for bathers. Thankfully, he had the common sense to take his teeth out and hand them to Richard Jones before taking the plunge. Egged on by the rest of the squad, Roger swam out to sea and then back again. As he got back on the coach and declared himself the winner of the money, he realised that he didn't have a towel. Although the weather was seasonally hot that day, the sea was not and the hapless Roger had to freeze as the bus made its way to the hotel where they were staying.

A less enjoyable experience for Roger during the 1995/96 season was having to endure a short period of being out of favour. Swansea's reserve 'keeper was Lee Jones – a player that Roger firmly believes was, and still is, a quality goalkeeper. Roger has never minded having competition for his place, as it helps keep him on top of his game. Lee had come into the side for a cup fixture in which the Swansea management had decided to drop their first-choice custodian. As Roger watched the game against Torquay, he knew would have a fight on his hands to get his jersey back as Lee played really well that night. The following game was away at Blackpool and it came as no surprise to Roger to find out that Lee had been picked to start the match. As it turned out, Roger's time out of the side did not last very long. Frank was displeased with Lee's performance during the first half and just before the interval Roger was told to warm up. He knew exactly how Lee would feel at being replaced at half time, but also knew that he had to look after number one and was not going to argue with Frank's decision. The Blackpool game was to be the last real chance of an extended spell of first-team football at Swansea for Lee Jones, who is now at Stockport and performing well.

By the end of the 1995/96 season, Swansea had secured another season of Division Two football. As the team went into the summer break, they could look back on their performances with a degree of satisfaction. However, as they left the Vetch that May, none of them could have guessed what was round the corner at Swansea City.

Roger pictured with a team mascot. Fearless Frank Burrows looks on.

8

RELEGATION WITH BURROWS, SMITH, RIMMER CULLIS AND MOLBY

At every level of the game comes the heartache of failing to achieve and the overall feeling of having let everyone down. During his career, Roger had already suffered from the feeling of loss that relegation brings about. A far greater loss was to come to him in the 1995/96 season, as not only were the Swans relegated to the basement division, but the saviour of Roger's career, Frank Burrows, left the club. 'Frank Burrows saved my career, when he signed me for Swansea I was at a low point, it wasn't Chelsea's fault, but I was desperate for a move back to Wales. When Swansea came in for me I was really excited that this would come true. But when he left Swansea I was very down, you could see that things were not going right for him, but I felt that he could have turned it round. I don't like to see managers sacked – well not all of them, there have been exceptions – but on the whole Frank did not warrant the stick he got. He walked, and as a player I was gutted.'

The relationship between Frank Burrows and Roger Freestone was very important to Roger. Unfortunately, the fans felt that Burrows had lost the plot. This came to a head during an away fixture at Burnley, when the travelling Swans support left everyone in no doubt that they wanted Frank to go. Roger saw things differently. He had worked with Frank and owed him so much for bringing him back to Wales. It therefore came as a blow to Roger in particular when Frank Burrows resigned his position and walked away from the club. Even the manager's close friends at the club were not aware that this would happen. Roger speculates 'I don't know if Frank had a ding-dong with Doug Sharpe or not, but the departure was very quick. Nobody expected this to happen, least of all me. We never really started a season off well, and I just felt we would turn it round.'

Burrows' departure during the 1995/96 saw Bobby Smith take charge at The Vetch. This period of Swansea's history and Roger's career is somewhat bleak. After Smith had taken up the reins, an indifferent run of form before Christmas saw the club slip down the division, and become firmly embroiled in a relegation battle. Morale was very low among the players. Roger describes the time, 'I just felt that things were not at all right. We had Robin Sharpe behind the scenes, and that was going to blow up in Bobby's face when he apparently asked for all weather boots for the players. There was an argument of some sort – and all that Bobby was trying to do was get us some decent kit, but for some reason it wasn't allowed to happen. Again, one minute he was here and then he was gone too. Two managers gone in a short space of time. It just wasn't the right way to run things; players need stability, and first Frank going, then Bobby, was very bad for the club. That is the real reason that Swansea were relegated that season.'

Bobby Smith's Christmas departure in 1995 sent the club into turmoil. For the second time that season, players were asking what was going on. Fortunately, senior professionals like David Penney and Keith Walker came to the fore 'Dave and Keith were the motivators at this point, and as the season progressed they took more of a role in the dressing room. With Bobby gone, it was obvious that Jimmy Rimmer was to take over, and I didn't think it was the right choice. We were scraping around looking for a few League points, and Jimmy was never the best person to talk to – he was very deep at times. And Jimmy, being an honest man, would tell you that coaching-wise he was not on a par with either Bobby or Frank. Jimmy's goal-keeping methods were very old school. I wasn't a big fan, and away from this area we needed serious guidance. Jimmy was probably one of Swansea's best ever goalkeepers, but for me he wasn't a manager on his own.'

Rimmer recognised that he needed assistance and sent for help in the form of Ken Mcnaught, an old Aston Villa team-mate. Immediately, Swansea City had some more belief as their off-the-field activities changed from Rimmer's old school methods. There was, however, more tension to come. Doug Sharpe was desperate to sell the club, with his son, Robin, taking more and more of a prominent role whilst his father sold the club he had supported man and boy to Michael Thompson. Thompson was a West Midlands businessman. In Jack Walker's son he had an avenue to loan money to set about buying the club and installing a manger.

This move would later cause the Swansea fans a great deal of anguish and embarrassment. For the players it was a disaster. Thompson came to an agreement with Doug Sharpe, which led to his brief ownership of The Swans. He immediately installed another West Midlands man as manager, Kevin Cullis. Allegedly the Cradely Town youth team manger at the time, Cullis was to manage a Football League side. Roger recalls this episode, 'The players were totally horrified when Cullis was appointed. We had just lost 3-0 at Stockport and the weather was bad. I phoned in to tell the club I couldn't get in for training the next day. I spoke to Emma Boat, and she told me that we had appointed a new manager. I got all excited, and as ever the talk was still about new stadiums and all that. I thought "Great, a new manager, maybe now we will get somewhere" as it had not been at all good since Frank left. Emma told me that the youth team manager from Cradely Town had been appointed. I laughed, I thought she was joking.'

The appointment of Kevin Cullis was no joke. Jimmy Rimmer was to remain, and Paul Molesworth, a respected scout in football circles, was to join Cullis at the Swansea helm. With two days to go before a crucial League fixture at home to Swindon, the squad trained on two inches of snow on astroturf at the Morfa Stadium. Rimmer took the training session as Cullis surveyed his new charges for the first time. Walking the touchline and already looking out of his depth, Cullis monitored not only the abilities of the squad, but also their value. Paul Molesworth takes up the story. 'Thompson asked me to have a look at the players and see who could be sold. I found this a bit worrying. There wasn't a great deal of money in the team, maybe Edwards, Torpey, Price and Freestone, but little else. I had moved from the Midlands to Swansea, my house was up for sale and we were actively looking for a new one. My wife is a school teacher and she was also about to hand in her notice. The money wasn't brilliant, but it was a golden opportunity to get into League football, and although Cullis was not a man I liked, I just went for it – who wouldn't?'

Molesworth was already a passing acquaintance of Cullis when he took the post. He talks of their first meeting, 'We had a player at Liverpool, who I was working for at the time, and Cullis got involved with the transfer – basically he messed it up. He put the young lad on a contract at Cradely, then thought he could ask for a fee. It all went flat for the youngster, and that was basically how I knew Cullis. I didn't like him that much to be honest. However, I was asked to get involved, and I was put on a contract, but as I said what worried me was Thompson looking to sell the best players straightaway. I just knew there was a money issue here, and as it transpired there was. Dougie wouldn't have known this at the time, but he was an astute man with Swansea at heart, and he quickly found out what Thompson was up to. They had a clause in the sale agreement that meant that if certain things did not happen then the £100,000 bond given to Dougie would stay with him, and Thompson would lose it. This, of course, happened in time.'

Roger recalls that first training session, 'He came to see us afterwards and said that we had played the best he had seen us in a long time – he must have seen some games – and it was the worst training session I had seen in years. All the lads looked at each other and sniggered, I thought that he knew little about the game anyway, and this just confirmed it. He really didn't know football players at this level. The next day after training, another session Cullis didn't take – in fact he never even took a team talk – he said to me, "Are you going to play a few rounds of golf now Roger?" I was appalled at this comment, any real manager would not have said that twenty-four hours before a game. I do not take alcohol at the best of times, and as for playing golf, another tiring activity the day before a big match … it was a ridiculous comment to make.' Roger immediately made it known to Cullis that he did not rate him as a manager. Informing his new boss that professional players rested before a big League game, he went back home to Risca. 'I am my own man, I don't go with the pack, I am not a boozer or a person who likes cliquey circles. I finish training and go home. If there is no game the next day I get in my mate's lorry and deliver goods in Birmingham to earn a few extra pounds, and get some time on my own. It whiles away a few hours and I love driving big lorries – it's a kid thing for me, so that's what I do. What I don't do is get drunk, play golf and get involved in all the other footballing pastimes that you read about. Cullis made me really angry when he said this, and it confirmed to me that he was completely out of his depth.'

Luckily for Swansea, Paul Molesworth also recognised the club's lack of direction under Cullis and contacted an old Anfield friend, Jan Molby. 'I could see that Cullis was out of his depth, he hadn't taken any training – that was Jimmy Rimmer's job – so what was he doing there? None of it felt right, and we had a massive game against Swindon coming up which we had to win. I got a hold of Jan and said get down to Swansea, it's a big club just itching for someone like you to get involved.'

Molby duly appeared that Saturday and was pictured clutching a match-day programme in Swansea's centre stand. But Jan was only there as a potential player. He takes up the story himself, 'Yeah, I went down to Swansea, just to see what was happening. I had been asked to go and I went. I was looking for a club, my Liverpool contract was up, and I had been on loan at Norwich and Barnsley, but nothing was doing at the time, so I went to Swansea.' Molby's brief appearance was a PR coup for Cullis and Thompson, as it gave the Swansea public hope and themselves a bit of credibility. Molesworth was not happy though, 'That was the problem, Jan being there was nothing at all to do with them, but they were milking it and swanning around talking real rubbish. I was worried. We had just lost to Swindon and looking in real danger, all they wanted to do was dine out on Jan Molby being there. What did it for me was the Welsh papers lapping it up and taking pictures of Cullis in the centre stand – they must have fell for it all hook, line and sinker.'

With the picture looking bleaker, and Doug Sharpe looking for his final instalment from Thomson, another crucial game against Blackpool loomed on the horizon. Roger was suffering from an abscess and Keith Walker was injured. Cullis appointed Roger as team captain for the day. It was a painful time. 'I was suffering badly from the abscess, and Cullis spoke to both me and Christian Edwards before the game. He offered us both four- and five-year contracts, but of course they never materialised. We went on to lose the game 4-0 and Dai Penney took the team talk. The reason for this was that Cullis didn't have a clue what he was talking about. It was a heated dressing room I can tell you, and Cullis was best out of the way. I don't think he would have been well received in there, lets just say that.'

What the Swansea players didn't know was that Doug Sharpe had been busying himself assessing Thompson's businesses and Kevin Cullis's football knowledge before the real sale of the club. The upshot was a car chase up the M6 to Blackpool on that dreary Tuesday night with Doug Sharpe confronting Thompson in a service station and telling him to get rid of Kevin Cullis. Paul Molesworth remembers it well, 'Dougie was fuming – he could see that Cullis was not fit for the position and told Thompson in no uncertain terms. It was very chilling. Thompson was clearly terrified of Dougie and lost his bottle completely. I can say this now, I am just glad Thompson took Dougie for real: I know he wanted rid of the club, but you must remember that Doug was a Swansea fan too, he didn't like what he was seeing, and sorted it out in a very basic way. As I said, Thompson was petrified.'

Roger remembers the moment that Doug Sharpe reintroduced himself to the players after the game against Blackpool. 'The coach doors flew open and there was Mr Sharpe. I thought we had seen the last of him. It's funny now, but at the time he looked like he could do murder. He just said, "Those two arseholes will be gone in the morning, trust me boys, they are history". I have to say I felt quite lifted by it all, and with Doug back it gave us renewed hope, especially as he had done a deal to bring Jan Molby to the club as player-manager. That was a great move, and typical of Doug Sharpe, he loved the club that was for sure.' Doug Sharpe had indeed taken back the club he loved and saved it from ruin.

Molesworth remained at the club in a scouting capacity, and eventually left the club on good terms. 'Doug is a fair man. He was a bit suspicious of me at first, but Jan put him straight, and I worked for Swansea for quite a long time, even when Silver Shield came in at Swansea I continued as a scout. I eventually moved on after the civil action Cullis brought against the club for unfair dismissal. Silver Shield took that case on as they were the new owners; Cullis was paid off, a few grand or so, I don't know, and that was that. All I can say about my time at Swansea was it was a real eye-opener, and not for the fainthearted. Thompson didn't have the cash to complete the deal for the club, and wanted to sell players off to do so. What is chilling is the fact that his backer would have coughed up the cash if it all hadn't been so underhand and secret. What would have happened to Swansea then? Personally speaking, it was better off back in Doug Sharpe's hands, and there can't be too many who would disagree with that.'

The club's antics off the field of play had certainly interfered with performances on it, and Swansea were now in a desperate fight for Division Two survival. The arrival of Molby was a massive boost for the club and gates rose as a result. Roger at last found the stability he and his colleagues craved. 'Jan just brought us together immediately. You could see he was a real winner and a genius with the ball. He oozed confidence, which rubbed off on everyone – at York City he brought the ball down in front of me and flicked it to one side, beating the striker in the six-yard box. That was the level of his play, brilliant.'   Sadly for Jan Molby and the club, Swansea were already effectively doomed to the drop as a result of bad feeling off the pitch and several managers who had already failed to achieve that season. Whilst it is impossible to lay a finger on the definitive cause of the rot, there are a number of factors that can be identified, including Doug Sharpe's insistence that he wanted to sell the club, Burrows, Smith, Cullis and Rimmer taking turns at the helm and the players having to take team talks when the manager couldn't. In all, Swansea were on a hiding to nothing in 1995/96. Molby did give the team hope, as a run of wins and draws saw them creep close to safety, but the writing was on the wall.

On another cold Tuesday night the side were relegated after losing miserably at Notts County. Molby looked to managing the side in Division Three and the future, while the Swansea fans and players looked back on one of the most embarrassing chapters in the club's history. It is safe to say that once again Doug Sharpe had saved the club, as he had helped to do in 1985, but this time he wanted out and the summer recess would see him still trying to offload the club.

Roger sums up the end of the season, 'We were genuinely down at the end of that season. Jan had come so close to keeping us up, and I looked at any number of given results that could have saved us, but it was not to be. Cullis was the final nail in the coffin, but what went on before was equally as bad. If Frank Burrows had stayed there we may have stayed up, but what would he have made of Cullis and Thompson? To be honest, when you think about Frank and his temper it's probably best that he left – I think he would still be kicking the pair of them up and down the Mumbles Road now if he had stayed at Swansea.'

9

SO NEAR BUT SO FAR

Love or hate the play-offs, they are part of a Nationwide season. Dreams of a Wembley final spur players on when their season is extended by a maximum of three games, and the heartache of losing in such a situation cannot be equalled by any other League defeat. During the 1990s, Swansea made two play-off appearances, and Roger played his part in both. Neither produced the desired result as far as the player and his club were concerned, but both are part of the Roger Freestone story. After the pain of relegation in 1996, Swansea entered the following season full of optimism. The players and fans felt that in Jan Molby they had the right man to lead them straight back to Division Two. After a slow start to the season, Swansea made moves in the right direction up the table and were keeping pace with the other leaders of the Division Three pack – a group of clubs which included their nearest rivals, Cardiff City.

There was a massive crowd at the Vetch as Swansea entertained Carlisle, who were also pushing at the top end of the table. Despite the 1-0 reverse, the football being played by Molby's Swansea deserved to grace a higher division. Roger puts much of this down to the influence of Jan himself. The Dane had won almost everything at club level and this was setting the tone for his first managerial job. Naturally, the players had a great respect for him, and held him in the same sort of esteem as Roger had Frank Burrows.

Molby recalls that first full season as Swans boss, 'I couldn't do much to save the club from relegation when I came to Swansea, but I knew I could do much better with a full run-up to the new season, and with my own thoughts on the team being put into place. I was new to being in charge, but I had my Liverpool ways with me that would surely rub off on the younger players like Lee Jenkins – and they did. I must not forget the contribution of Billy Ayre either, he was the best right-hand man you could wish for. Swansea did not have quality in depth but they did have a very good youth system, something I concentrated on a lot, and there were players there who could go on and have a very healthy career in football. I've mentioned Lee Jenkins, but there was others, and they were going to be Swansea's future. I felt very responsible to all of them, and took the Swansea job very personally. Looking back at it now, there was very little I would have done differently, we were a good side that had been neglected – but many had Frank Burrows' stamp on them, which meant good football.

And good football was going to get us through it, or so I thought.'

Molby was another manager that the players did not want to get on the wrong side of. Because of this 'fear factor', the players would often dig in and find that extra bit to produce results from nowhere. Swansea were able to give the top teams in the division a really good test, as they proved against Fulham on a Tuesday night. Fulham were the leaders of the division and had all but assured themselves promotion very early on. Swansea were a match for them, however, despite eventually losing 2-1 after taking the lead. Roger realised that although they were set for the play-offs rather than automatic promotion, the team stood a very good chance of reaching their ultimate goal and being promoted.

Swansea's play-off place was guaranteed before the last game of the season against Darlington. Roger was rested for the match to save his energy for the play-off battle, Lee Jones standing in for him. Molby did not tell Roger that he was being rested. The former Liverpool star believed that, as manager, it was his right to select the team and not have to justify his selections. As Roger watched the last game of the regular season, he was anxious about his place in the side and whether he was in the manager's plans for the next match. Roger need not have worried, he was very much in Jan's plans for the play-offs and rated highly by the Dane: 'Roger was the number one at Swansea, he was capable and sound, and his reaction saves at times were brilliant. You wouldn't have picked a Swansea team at that time without including Roger Freestone. He may have thought I had dropped him, but we were already secure in the play-off's – so why risk him?'

Swansea headed into the play-offs with Northampton Town, Cardiff City and their opponents in the semi-final, Chester City. The appearance of Cardiff in the other semi-final was one of concern for the Football League. Since the incidents of a few years previous, away supporters had been banned from the games between the two clubs, and the thought of 50,000 or more fans from the two clubs at Wembley stadium was a major security headache for the authorities. The significance of the situation was not lost on the Swansea supporters either, and there was much talk was about possible meeting with their rivals at the home of football.

Thoughts of playing in the final against anyone were put out of the players' minds as they prepared for the games against Chester. The first leg was to be played at Chester the following Sunday, and Jan was again trying to bring some of his Liverpool pedigree into the preparations. Jan was aware of what worked well at football clubs. Liverpool had been immensely successful over the previous twenty years, and the manager believed that he could use that recipe for that success at Swansea. Part of the formula was proper preparation for a big game. Although Chester is on the Welsh/English border, Jan took his team up for the game on the Friday morning. He reasoned that in doing this he would take his players away from much of the reports and speculation that surrounded the game, allowing them to fully concentrate on the task ahead.

As the squad travelled north, Roger gratefully received confirmation that he was still in the manager's plans when he read a quote from Jan about the game which included the words 'I have every faith in Roger'. Swansea trained on the Friday afternoon and Saturday morning, and went into the first game in good shape. As Roger himself admits, the first leg match was a boring game. There were no real chances for either side and it came as little surprise to the fans that the score was 0-0 after 90 minutes.

Again breaking from the norm, Jan kept his players in Chester for another overnight stop on the Sunday, rather than immediately travelling back home. The Swansea players were satisfied that they had done a good job in securing the draw from the first game, but were warned that the result on the following Wednesday was far from secured. After heading back into Wales on the Monday, the players were allowed to spend the afternoon and evening with their families. Jan wanted them all back together the following day to prepare for the second game, and the team reunited in Llanelli for an overnight stay on the Tuesday.

Training on the Tuesday and Wednesday was held at Stebonheath Park, home of Llanelli Football Club. It was a relaxed and confident Swansea side that arrived at the Vetch to try and secure the club's second appearance at Wembley. As the players got ready in the dressing room, the noise from the terraces that was filtering through was incredible. Roger thought that it was the most electric atmosphere he had ever been in as he ran out onto the pitch, a feeling that was confirmed as the full house at the Vetch Field created an intimidating atmosphere for the opposition. Despite the fervent support, Swansea did not to have the best start to the game, although the setback did not come in the form of a Chester goal.

Swansea's regular right-back was Steve Jones, a player who had given his all for Swansea since signing from Cheltenham Town. 'Jonah' was one of Roger's closest friends at Swansea, as he lived in Gloucester and the two men travelled to training together most days. As Jones went down after a collision, Roger ran to attend to him and was greeted with a sight that haunts him to this day. His friend had clearly broken his leg and it was not a nice sight. The game was held up for quite a while as Jonah was attended to and then carried off to hospital. Although a major blow to Swansea, the incident gave them extra determination to win the game for the sake of their stricken team-mate. Roger recalls the moment he saw his best friend's leg in pieces, 'I couldn't look at it, it was awful – one of the worst sights any professional player could see. I remember seeing Peter Schmiecal run away in terror when David Busst the Coventry player ended his career in a penalty box collision, it was just like that. Kwame Ampadu had put in a hard tackle on an incoming Chester player in the box, as did Steve. They both went for the same ball. The players clashed, and Steve's leg ripped backwards – it was immediately clear to me that he was in a lot of trouble. I cannot describe those few moments, his leg was just facing the other way and twisted. It was absolutely sickening, the foot facing one way and his knee the other – it makes me sick now to think about it, just smashed to pieces. Then an ambulance was on the pitch and Steve was being placed very carefully in to the back of it. There were 10,000 Swans fans there that night, and you could hear a pin drop when Steve was put in to the back of that ambulance. It was horrifying.'

Jones faced months of uncertainty as he rehabilitated himself to full fitness, and he would miss all of the next season. The truth only came out much later that he was literally minutes away from having his leg amputated. Jones was Roger's rock at the back and was sadly missed. Jones has particularly harrowing memories of the incident, 'When my leg went I was certain that I had ended my career. There were players all about me and I could hear the comments, then I was out of it. I cannot remember anything else. It wasn't painful as much as the shock. I was up for the biggest game of my career, and I knew we would win. That meant I would be playing at Wembley, in front of thousands, then in a moment it was over and I wouldn't play football for sixteen months. I was crushed, totally wiped out. It was an awful time for me, and the worst moment in my career as a professional.'

Swansea went on to win the game easily 3-0, David Thomas heading a crucial goal to send the North Bank wild. The Swans were heading for a second Wembley appearance in three years. In the other semi-final, Northampton Town had defeated Cardiff City and were to provide the opposition. Despite the loss of a potential Wembley derby, there was also a sense of relief in the Swansea camp that all attention was now going to be on the game rather than the supporters – and, of course, a number of police forces were happy as well.

The build up to the play-off final was more relaxed than the previous visit to the famous stadium, and Swansea stayed at the England training complex before the game. The usual pre-Wembley build-up took place, including the suit fitting – for which, as Roger puts it, they do make them in extra large! The squad travelled up for the game, which was to take place on the Saturday of the May Bank Holiday weekend. On the Thursday they took part in a couple of training sessions as well as the odd snooker or pool tournament among themselves.

As with the last trip, Ken was again the bus driver, but this time there were no Freestone tricks for him to endure. Swansea were favourites for the game, as they had a highly experienced League squad. One of the players at the time was Linton Brown. Roger remembers him as a player who had the ability but, for whatever reason, did not seem to want to play football. There was one occasion at Ninian Park where Linton was due to play as there had been a squad injury. Surprisingly, Linton claimed to have developed an injury during the warm-up for the game and was unable to take part. Roger was convinced that this was a contrived excuse to avoid the match 'Linton was pulling a fast one, that's for sure. He was in the side for the big derby game, and there were many players just itching for a chance to have a go at Cardiff City. Linton just didn't have it in him at all. He could have ripped them apart, he was that sort of player. It seemed to me that he was scared of the fight we were going to have with Cardiff City, and in my mind he wasn't needed if that was the case. But on occasion, Linton would be on form and really up for it.

He had some games where he was the star, he would put his head down and run his heart out for Swansea. But when he was needed against Cardiff he failed to respond – he was better off out of it and away from the game.'

There were other players in the team that Roger unconditionally rated. John Hodge, Carl Heggs and Steve Torpey were particularly highly thought of by Roger and, although there was no complacency in the side, the team was confident that they could deliver the required result and bring Division Two football to Swansea for the following season. Roger remembers John Hodges with particular warmth: 'Hodgey was a comic, but on his day he could put in the best cross that any goalkeeper could try and deal with. Pure class was Hodgey. He scored some stunning goals for Swansea, and when he left it was a shame. However, I thought that would be the end of him, he had this self destruct button in him. But he went on to much better things away from Swansea, which did surprise me a lot. Not that he didn't have the talent, it was just that he was a bit mad, on and off the pitch. But he was a real team player, and the sort of lad you needed in the dressing room when things were getting tasty. He would inspire players and give the ones with nerves that extra edge. We needed that inspiration during this time at Swansea.'

As the two sides lined up to be led out onto the pitch, Roger found himself next to John Gayle, Northampton's towering striker. Roger had been through a fair few tussles with John over the years and decided that it was time to prompt a pre-match discussion with him. 'Hey John, no elbows today please' was Roger's comment, to which John looked at him blankly and said 'I'll play the game as I fucking want to'. There was, however, no malice in this exchange – just two players exchanging a bit of banter.

As it turned out, Christian Edwards, Swansea's central defender, was to have John in his pocket all afternoon and Gayle's elbows were not in evidence at all during the game. Both sides were reasonably well-matched throughout the game and, with extra time looming, the score was still 0-0. Northampton won a free-kick on the edge of the Swansea penalty area and Roger lined up his wall for one last piece of defensive work before the conclusion of normal time. The kick was taken, but blocked by the Swansea wall and cleared. Before the Swansea players could congratulate themselves on a job well done, however, the referee blew his whistle and booked a defender for encroaching on the kick. Swansea re-worked their plan and changed the player assigned with charging the kick to Jonathan Coates. The position of the free-kick was also slightly moved, but Roger was still confident that they would block it and keep their season alive. John Frain aligned himself and struck the ball as Coates made the decision to move towards him. If he had stayed in the wall, the kick would have hit him on the chest, but his decision to charge and duck was a crucial one as Frain's shot nestled in the bottom right-hand corner of Roger's net.

Roger was left without any feeling at all. Such numbness was something that he had not experienced before on the football pitch. Swansea were a goal down with little, if any, time to try and rectify the situation. The players returned to the centre circle to kick off and the referee's whistle blew for full-time. Jan and his players sank to their knees in disbelief. They were beaten and had no chance to pull it back. They had played 49 League games since the previous August, and it had all come to nothing with the final kick of the season. Although it was hard work for all of them, Molby wanted his players to acknowledge the support that they had received, not only in that game but over the previous nine months. Despite feeling devastated, Roger and the rest of the team took the sympathetic support of their fans while the Northampton team and supporters celebrated at the other end.

It took a while to get over that defeat, not only for Roger but for the rest of the team. There were no retributions against any one individual or team meetings to work out where it went wrong, but a unilateral feeling of dismay went through the squad. Roger had never felt anything like this after losing a game before and it was several weeks into the summer break before he came to terms with the cruel way in which his season had finished. Following his second play-off failure in a Swansea shirt, Roger wondered if he would ever experience joy in such a situation. He was to get another chance two years later at the end of another very eventful season.

Memories of the nearly show at Wembley and Jan Molby dropping to his knees at the final whistle were quickly forgotten as the race to sell Swansea City began in earnest. Doug Sharpe was now committed to selling the club and among rumours of multi-million pound consortiums there was only one real sale to be made – to Silver Shield owner Neil McClure. Little was known about the man at the time and he was fronted by Steve Hamer, London Sporting Club share holder and a local boy from Neath. Hamer could talk the talk and McClure gave the air that he knew what was required to carry the team forward. Over the summer, however, Dave Penney, Carl Heggs and Steve Torpey left – the lattermost for a fee of £400,000 to Bristol City.

Hamer proved his Swansea City credibility with tales of the 1960s, when Swansea had hooped socks and little else to worry about. He also professed experience of playing in the Welsh Football League. Roger recalls the appointment of the new men at the top. 'It was another real time of change for us, but they seemed to know what they were on about on the face of it. But, like many others, I had my doubts, and the fans clearly had theirs too. But you give people a chance, and they did unveil grand plans of a 25,000 all-seater stadium and Premiership football in five years. So I thought it was worth hanging about. Of course they were soon found out and became a bit of a laughing stock in time.'

Steve Hamer takes up the story. 'Yes hands up, we handled it poorly and maybe some of the people involved underestimated the Swansea people – I should have been wiser to it but I wasn't. I let my heart rule my head at times, and McClure employed people like Mike Lewis, on my say so, as chairman, and brought in the likes of Peter Day and Phil Chant. All of them were capable, but in Lewis' case he came as commercial manager on good recommendation – what he was not was a potential managing director. McClure appointed him later on in capacities that I was only made aware of after the event. This didn't do my relationship with McClure any good at all, and in time was the downfall of my position and indeed the reason why he did not build a stadium, and bring about anything he really wanted to do.'

Within a few games of the 1997/98 season, Jan Molby was sacked and reasons given ranged from the fact he had lost the plot to a loss of respect from the players. However, Roger puts that immediately to rest, 'No way did Jan lose any respect from any of us, he was sacked far too early in the season and the real reason, in my opinion, was his salary and his position with the supporters. They loved him – it was total adoration – and the players, especially the youngsters, were flourishing under his guidance. He was a great manager, and should have been given the time he deserved. It does make you angry when compared to the John Hollins scenario – Molby would never have been given the chances he had. That's the annoying thing about it all.

A 7-4 defeat at Hull City signalled the end for Molby in real terms and, within a day, Mickey Adams was appointed manager with Alan Cork as his assistant. 'We were all over the place,' recalls Roger. 'Mickey knew what he wanted to do, but we didn't have the fitness for his type of game – I could see he had the heart and was a very good manager, he has proved that since, but something just wasn't right.'

Adams left the club after thirteen days and has never made a statement on the real reasons why.

Alan Cork took over and although his record was not brilliant, he did bring players to the club who have stabilised matters since and earned the club a divisional title eighteen months later. Matthew Bound was one who signed from Stockport County in a £50,000 deal. 'I was delighted to go to Swansea – it's very different there to anywhere else I have been, the fans are magnificent and the noise they make is incredible. Swansea relaunched my career and gave me some real goals as a player, it is a great place to play football.' Jason Smith was also captured for a minimal fee from Tiverton Town and midfield dynamo

Roger poses for a publicity shot with Kwame and Carl.

Martin Thomas also came in to harden up a side lacking aggression in crucial areas of the pitch.

The season was not going at all well for Cork, who Swans fans found hard to understand after such a good relationship with Molby. The League position reflected a side in turmoil and Cork even found himself going head to head with Swans fans in the main stand as defeats increased the pressure on him. A few months earlier the side was at Wembley in a play-off final, now they were staring at the bottom of Division Three. Respite was earned at Ninian Park with a wonder goal from Keith Walker as The Swans beat their bitter rivals 1-0, live on Sky TV, but the writing was on the wall. Swansea had to just survive the season and a massive rethink would have to take place.

With the promises of a new stadium proven false time and time again, a lowly League position saw the inevitable departure of Alan Cork from the club and the appointment of a man who Steve Hamer knew very well indeed from his London connections. One time Chelsea European Cup Winner John Hollins was announced to South Wales as the man to lead the club forward to greater things. If Swans fans though that the past few years had been a roller-coaster they could never have predicted the next few. The John Hollins years had arrived.

Memories of the Jan Molby play-off season at Wembley. Pictured with Roger are, from right to left: Carl Heggs, Colin Pascoe and Kwame Ampadu.

10

HEROES AND VILLAINS

The 1998/99 season was one that Swansea fans would remember very well. With a new manager at the helm in John Hollins, hopes were high that Swansea could mount a serious promotion campaign. The season started brightly and Swansea were in a respectable league position when the FA Cup first round brought a home tie against Millwall. Having enjoyed a few decent FA Cup runs in his career, this was one of the hardest ties that Roger and Swansea could have got in the opening rounds, with Millwall flying high near the top of Division Two. However, the Lions were to prove no match for Swansea, who destroyed them in the first half with a magnificent display to secure a 3-0 victory and a second round draw against Stoke City.

If the first round had given Swansea a tough draw, the second round was even harder. Stoke were even further up the table than Millwall, although Swansea found themselves 1-0 up at the interval. Roger was aware that he could expect an onslaught during the second half, and so it proved as he had to withstand one of the hardest 45 minutes he had known. Stoke threw everything at Roger's goal but he and his fellow defenders stood firm to hold the advantage.

Swansea were in the third round of the FA Cup again, and the following day Roger watched the television closely as they followed West Ham United out of the hat. A plumb tie at Upton Park was a suitable reward for two very good displays from John Hollins' team, and a superb way in which to start 1999.

There was the little matter of a few League games to negotiate first, but it did not seem too long before Swansea's travelling fans headed into London for the big game. This was also to be the occasion on which they were introduced to John Hollins' subsequent away-game habit of draping a Welsh flag over the visitors' dugout. Patriotic pride seemed to do the trick as Roger and Swansea not only matched, but also outplayed, their more illustrious opponents and deservedly went in front midway through the second half, Jason Smith heading them into the lead. One of the big upsets of that season was on the cards. West Ham duly went in search of the equaliser and pushed hard, but found it very difficult to break down the Swansea defence. With just three minutes to play, disaster struck Swansea City and Roger in particular. Julian Dicks, a left-back with a hard-man reputation, took a pot shot at the goal from outside the penalty area. There seemed little danger as Roger went to gather the ball, but somehow the shot went through him. The look of horror on Roger's face said it all as the ball nestled in the back of the net. He was devastated. The side had played so well and he had given away a soft goal to let the Premiership team back into the tie.

It was all very hard for Roger to take in as the final whistle blew. His mistake had probably cost Swansea a prominent place on the back pages of the following day's papers, although he was helped by the support of his team-mates, who were only too happy to console him for his mistake. John Hollins reassured his side that they had played well and that this was now only half time in the tie. Despite such reassurances, Roger vowed that he would atone for his mistake.

Swansea's preparations for the replay were disrupted by a poor 4-0 League defeat at Exeter City, before all eyes focused on their second attempt to overpower the Premiership giants. The following Wednesday dawned with rain pouring down over Swansea, but the city was gripped by cup fever. Queues of people had been outside the Vetch the week before trying to get their hands on the tickets for the game and the match was officially a sell out.

Roger's mind was always focused before big games, but tonight it was even more so because of his mistake at Upton Park. He knew that the continuing rain and heavy pitch would give the home side some assistance on the evening and that this could be the night for a giant-killing. Swansea were given the perfect start to the game when Martin Thomas scored a goal, to the delight of the huge home crowd. Again, West Ham surged forward in search of the equaliser but Swansea's defence once more held firm.

With the tie once again heading towards injury time, and West Ham still looking for the equaliser, another player with a 'hard man' reputation took a shot at goal. Every person in the crowd believed, because of ferocity and accuracy of the strike, that Swansea were again to be denied the victory that their endeavours deserved. This time, however, Roger refused to be beaten and he flew across his goal to tip Ruddock's shot around the post and preserve Swansea's slender advantage. As the ball disappeared over the line for the corner, two of the home players sunk to their knees and Martin Thomas later described it as 'the best save I have ever seen'. Chairman Hamer mentioned to Roger afterwards that he reminded him of Yashin, the famous Russian 'keeper – to which Roger looked at him and asked 'Did he play in black and white?' Following Roger's amazing save, Swansea clung on to their advantage to achieve one of the biggest upsets of the round. Their reward was a home tie against more Premiership opposition as they were drawn to face Derby County in the fourth round.

Another capacity crowd packed into the Vetch to see Derby scrape a 1-0 win with a goal in the last ten minutes. With the benefit of hindsight, Roger now admits that he should not have played in that game. His desperation to participate took over, however, and he was to pay the penalty by missing the next three League games with a ruptured disk in his back. Despite Roger's absence, Swansea retained their push for a play-off position, facing three games in five days in the final week of the season – away at Brentford, followed by home games against Cambridge United and Hull City. The first of these matches did not go well, with Swansea crashing to a 4-1 defeat against a side that would go on to win automatic promotion. This left Swansea two home games to secure an extension to the season. In the first of them, goals from Steve Watkin gave them a 2-0 victory, lifting the club into the play-off zone with just one game to go.

The final Saturday of the football season was welcomed into Swansea with more heavy rain. The Vetch pitch was almost underwater and the club applied to the Football League to let them postpone the fixture. Permission was refused, and as the ground staff tried to clear the water from the playing surface, the players tried to focus on the job ahead. The game eventually started later than those played elsewhere, giving Swansea the luxury of knowing the result they needed to take part in the play-offs. As it turned out, a Steve Watkin goal in both halves of the game gave them a 2-0 win and meant they would face Scunthorpe United to decide who would go to the Wembley final.

Roger thought about the play-offs in the week leading up to the first leg and, having already suffered two defeats in the-end-of-season lottery, he hoped that this was to be third time lucky and that he could finally celebrate his first promotion with the club.

The following Sunday it was back to the Vetch for the last home game of the season. Swansea had passed several stern tests during the campaign and Roger was hopeful that they could manage a good result. Matthew Bound scored a goal to put Swansea ahead, and they pressed for the second, Tony Bird hitting the post. The game ended 1-0 to Swansea. Although they were ahead, as the team prepared for the second leg Roger was only too aware that the one-goal advantage could be wiped out in seconds and that he had to be ready for an onslaught from Scunthorpe in second leg.

Sadly, the advantage was indeed quickly wiped out, as Steve Jones put the ball into his own net within the first few minutes of the game to give the home side the lead on the night and pull the scores level on aggregate. Tension was also mounting on the terraces, as the tie reached boiling point. Brian Laws, the Scunthorpe manager, had lit the blue touch paper before the game by placing an English flag in the centre circle of the pitch, prompting John Hollins to drape his Welsh flag on the dugout in response.

There were no more goals during the 90 minutes and both sides had to endure another thirty minutes of football. Scunthorpe grabbed an early goal to take the lead, but Swansea pulled a goal back from Steve Watkin and were back in front of the tie on the away goals rule. If they could have held on then it was another Wembley date for the team. Scunthorpe had other ideas, scoring again before holding out for a 3-2 aggregate win.

Despite being a third-time play-off loser, Roger still believed that the system had a place in deciding promotions. 'They keep the season alive for many clubs and, despite the fact that I am a three-time loser in them, all the clubs are aware at the start of the season that they will be there and that your season could end to a side that finished lower in the league than you. Having lost in two semi-finals and one final, I would say that any play-off defeat, from a personal point of view, hurts just as much and they are not a nice way to finish the season. If you finish just outside you realise that your league position was not good enough but to lose over either 90 or 180, or even 210 minutes, it is a hard feeling and you have all summer to ponder over what may have been.' At the end of 1998/99, Roger headed off on the summer break with the words of his manager in his mind – 'remember how hard this is to take and try to never get in this position again'.

11

CHAMPIONS HOLLINS STYLE

There was no getting away from it, John Hollins was starting the 1999/2000 season with a few points to prove. He had seen his side fall at the penultimate hurdle the season before, and didn't want to face the same scenario again. The only way to avoid the play-off drama with its nail-biting tension was to go up directly. With a trusty back four now in place – namely Steve Jones, Michael Howard, Jason Smith and Matthew Bound – Hollins had a defence capable of keeping goals conceded to a minimum. In midfield he had Nick Cusack, and players who, on their day, could put in a fine performance – Jon Coates, Damien Lacey, Lee Jenkins, Jason Price, Richie Appleby, Kris O' Leary, Ryan Casey and Stuart Roberts. Up front was the big frame of fans' plea signing Julian Alsop and Steve Watkin, although Hollins had little in reserve when it came to getting the goals. Chairman Steve Hamer also saw the deficiency of the attack 'It was clear that John needed more than we had up front, and he came to me and asked for some bolstering up front … We fished around and it came to our notice that an agent representing Jamaican international Walter Boyd was touting him around. That was Barri Mackintosh, he was well known in football circles. We decided to have a go at him as we were sure that Cyril the Swan was not going to get us up, no matter how much publicity he was getting at the time.'

The season started slowly. Peter Day, the chief executive, left at the end of July, much to the satisfaction of many Swans fans. He had not endeared himself to the supporters who stood upon the North Bank. The sentimental on the terraces were not happy that the club was being run by a conglomerate of outsiders. Furthermore, Hollins was clearly being told by Neil McClure that he had to get rid of players before purchasing, and with many on long-term contracts, that was not going to happen. What annoyed many fans was his constant talk of players coming in, when all around him knew it would never happen. The ficticious *South Wales Evening Post* writer Martin Pitchwell (who was in actual fact the editor George Edwards) reflected that no money spent meant no money wasted. That did nothing to appease the anger in the city, and in a way was a clever method of getting a point across without upsetting anyone. The local paper thrived on good communications with the club, and would not dare to question any of the incumbent regime.

Despite rumbles of discontent from the supporters, the season started well and the defence remained firm as two straight victories signalled some hope for promotion. An away win at Macclesfield sent the side straight in to the top six, Jason Price seeming to score at will from midfield. A League Cup victory over Millwall led to Hollins stating that 'Swansea were gathering a reputation', particularly in view of the FA Cup run of the season before.

September brought Walter Boyd to the city. The forward claimed that 35 goals would be his target for the season, and when he signed he even wore that squad number on his jersey. Such a boast proved hollow. As he would not manage even half of that target in two seasons at the club, only shining on the field when his confidence was high. To be fair to Boyd, however, he was never regularly selected by Hollins. Roger remembers Walter's arrival. 'He was a strange person I thought, very withdrawn and quiet, almost mute. But he was a nice guy, and when he did speak people tended to listen, and you could not doubt his quality. He was a legend in Jamaica – on a par with Bob Marley as a celebrity – but I hadn't heard of him before. Maybe that's my own fault or ignorance, but when he did take to the field against Rotherham at The Vetch he scored two goals on his debut, and that sent confidence soaring.'

Derby knocked Swansea out of the League Cup and during October the clouds increased over Vetch Field with goals at a premium. Although a four-goal salvo, against none other than Inter Cardiff, brought hope, it was short lived as Swansea continued to falter in front of goal. A small section of the supporters called for Hollins to go. The cries were premature, but the dissent coming from the supporters and constant rhetoric from the club was wearing everyone down, while Walter Boyd's work permit was a long time coming.

Amidst this strange climate, Roger signed an extension to his contract which took in his testimonial year, and brought an end (once again) to speculation that he was to join Bristol City. 'There was never any chance that I would go to Bristol City unless the club made it clear that they didn't want me at any level. I didn't want to go, and although a number of clubs were being mentioned, I had no intention of leaving. I was offered the one-year extension and straight away made it known in the press that Swansea was the place I wanted to stay. Again my family were the issue, and as there had been no concrete approach from Bristol City, I was not going to get all involved with the speculation. It would have been easier to sign for them, it's not too far away from home, and the money would have been better than the money that I was on at the time at Swansea. But I just didn't want to leave. I will admit that I did receive phone calls at home from both Bristol City and Cardiff City, but nothing came of them.'

Defeated against Hull in the League, the Swans turned around a one-goal deficit – a brilliant strike by Lua Lua – against Colchester in the FA Cup to progress once again. Unfortunately, Oldham Athletic despatched the side out of the FA Cup in the next round, Alsop and Boyd missed golden chances and 2,000 unhappy Swans fans endured the long, cold and quiet journey home.

The season progressed in fits and starts, with results getting poorer during November and December. After not getting the starts that everyone had hoped for, Boyd shot into the record books by being sent off against Darlington at the Vetch Field after a record nil seconds. Coming on as a substitute, he elbowed a Darlington player and was immediately despatched back to the bench. In the interim, a throw-in had yet to be taken – Walter making himself a newsworthy item as a 'bad boy' in the national press. Swansea were mid-table and looking hopeless, and as Christmas approached, a rumour circulated that Nick Cusack had actually saved Hollins' job by scoring the winner at Chester in a 1-0 victory. Following this result, almost miraculously, Swansea began to climb the table.

Morale at the club was still not great, however. Walter Boyd arrived a whole twenty minutes late for the home win over York City, infuriating John Hollins who reduced him to shivering in the stands. Hollins stated that he had not received any explanation for Boyd's lateness, and, quite rightly, disciplined him. But the team was gradually gaining momentum as the players rallied behind their manager to prove that they were indeed good enough. This point was proved, albeit in many rather boring encounters that showed The Swans to be a defensive unit to be reckoned with. By the end of the season, Roger and his defence would boast the best defensive record for the number of games played in the country, with only Liverpool even coming close.

A wonderful 3-2 victory at Peterborough, after the team was 2-0 down at half time, took some of the flack off the manager. After all the problems off the pitch, it was now a time for confidence. The Swans were on the trail of records, and a sequence of nine straight wins was there for the taking if they beat Macclesfield at The Vetch Field, which they duly did. Swansea City went to the top of the league, only to be removed when their away game at Carlisle was postponed, although local league side West End took some of the shine off the achievement when they despatched the Swans from the West Wales Senior Cup with a 2-0 defeat.

Things were taking shape at The Vetch, with attendances creeping up to respectable levels. A 4-1 thumping of Northampton Town was shown live on Sky TV, but 7,500 supporters still turned up at the ground – including 54 from Northampton. The Division Three championship was becoming a two-horse race between Rotherham United and Swansea City. It could not have been set up better – the League fixtures panel having creating a potentially monumental occasion with Swansea to play Rotherham at Millmoor on the last day of the season. Nobody could have predicted such a finale.

Nerves were stretched as 2,000 Swansea fans made the journey to Home Park, Plymouth. A 1-0 defeat provoked the wrong sort of reaction from the travelling support as Swansea City fans fought running battles after the game with police and home fans.

John Cornforth led an Exeter City side to The Vetch Field for the last home game of the season. Declaring his love for the club he led to Autoglass glory, he hoped that the club would win the championship. The fact that he could take that away from his former club by leading Exeter to victory was clearly tugging at his heart and perhaps a satisfactory draw would have suited both sides. However, in the early summer sun that shone over Swansea, Exeter City were hammered into the ground – a near-full house dancing and celebrating a stunning Jon Coates goal as a consummate team performance embarrassed Exeter City and their small band of loyal supporters.

The championship decider took place at Rotherham on Saturday 6 May 2000. 2,500 tickets were given to Swansea to sell to their army of fans, with coaches, mini-buses, trains and cars carrying the supporters to Yorkshire. Amongst the faithful was Terry Cole, a life-long Swans fan joining in the celebration of the promotion and the fact that Swansea City had a good chance of winning a divisional championship for the first time since 1949. Alan Curtis, the assistant manager, had even more to celebrate. A Swansea man through and through, his uncle, Roy Paul, was a part of the team that won that championship for City. The day was set for a massive game, but would end in disaster for Terry and his family, as events off the pitch took over the news headlines.

Terry was a Swansea nut, who loved to watch the side at home and away. His children, Matthew and Natalie, would also accompany him to games, and his bedroom at their family home was a shrine to Swansea City. He travelled with his friends to the game, and just after 2.15 p.m. made his way to the small alley that feeds away supporters at Rotherham in to the ground. Already there had been confrontation between a large group of Swansea supporters and Rotherham supporters in the road opposite. Rotherham police cells could hardly cope. As Terry made his way to the entrance of the alley, a hailstorm of bricks and bottles landed in the street. Police on horseback attempted to restore order, and Terry, a football fan and not at all involved in the trouble, found himself in the path of distressed horses and absolute mayhem. Terry was unable to avoid the crowds and the horses, and in a horrific moment was trampled under the hooves of a police horse. Suffering from extreme head injuries, he was taken to the local hospital at Rotherham where he later died. Little was known of the events outside the ground as Swansea fans squeezed down the alleyway, via the small gates, into the newly seated area that housed the away fans.

Many were aware that Swansea fans had been involved in bad scenes outside the ground, and rumour spread that a supporter had died. Confirmation is not possible, however, in such a heated atmosphere, and further confrontations on the back of the rumours was inevitable. The game was tense, and turned on an incident involving Jason Price in the penalty area in front of the Swans support. Jason was brought down and the referee immediately gave the penalty. Matthew Bound put The Swans 1-0 up. A draw would have been good enough, but with only a few minutes to go it confirmed Swansea as champions, hundreds of fans ran on to the pitch in celebration, with Rotherham supporters also coming onto the pitch to complicate matters. In the melee, Steve Jones was assaulted by a Rotherham fan, and after the game had restarted Rotherham were awarded a penalty. This was calmly put away to equalise proceedings between the two sides.

A further pitch invasion occurred, and lines of police fought to restore order in one of the most heated games Swansea City had played in for years. A further chance for the home side was spurned, and the game was ended after eight minutes of injury time. Celebrations commenced as the travelling Swans fans swarmed on to the pitch, to dance away the afternoon with John Hollins and his players. The Division Three trophy was given to Nick Cusack, and the traditional celebrations went on for some forty-five minutes. Swansea were champions.

Lessons to be learned were talked about by people in power, and FA spokesmen talked of the hindrance to England's World Cup bid. The gap between these people, and the real football fan could not have been wider. Tributes were paid, and some even felt that to apportion blame would be a good idea – indeed, the need to blame someone is often the way in times such as these. But neither Terry nor the police officer wanted this terrible thing to happen. The fact that it did puts everything to do with football and things that are said about it into a different context.

The season had ended on a deeply sad note. Roger's thoughts on this passage of Swansea history are unequivocal, 'I was so sad that Terry died, that goes without saying. If it meant he were alive today, and we were not to win the league or even go up then I would swap that now, no bother at all. Football means nothing compared to the loss his family must have felt since that day. I just wish the clock could be turned back.'

Swansea fans celebrate their team's triumph.

Freestone in goal for Swansea at the crucial championship encounter with Rotherham.

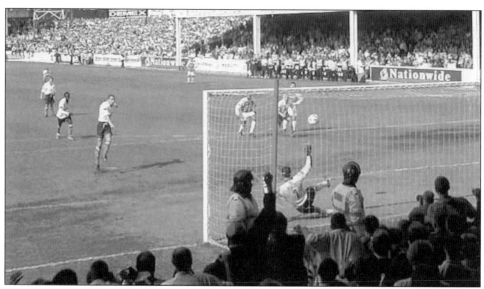

Matt Bound slams home the penalty.

Freestone and Cusack celebrate finishing the season as champions.

12

RELEGATION HOLLINS STYLE

At the end of the 2000/2001 season, Swansea once again found themselves back in Division Three. This time a plethora of managers was not the cause and many fans laid the blame squarely on John Hollins. Indeed, the manager would pay for it with his job when the 2001/02 was just a few weeks old. In May 2000, Swansea City were champions of Division Three after a remarkable season of 1-0 victories and backs-to-the-wall defending. The promise of new players over the summer was never realised and it was clear to most Swansea fans that the 2000/01 season would be a struggle.

Roger remained philosophical about the situation, 'Consolidate was the word we were using at the start of the 2000 season. We would never go up with the same squad as the season before, but never in a month of Sundays did I think we would go back down, that was a real shocker. I was surprised that we never made any real purchases until the season was well under way, Giovanni Savarese had come in and looked good, and although he wasn't getting games for us, Walter Boyd could have been one of the reasons why we could have stayed up. But he wasn't getting games – why I don't know, you can't doubt his quality, as he has proved himself on the international stage, but he never realised his potential at Swansea. I also thought we should have kept Julian Alsop, he terrifies defences and I don't relish coming up against him, but that's football and I have come to expect changes as and when they happen.'

Swansea started the campaign fairly well and looked as though they would be a good mid-table side come May 2001. Good results against Wigan, Stoke City and Bristol City displayed a side to Swansea City that few had seen in recent years. However, the failure to sign players in the summer was to come back and haunt both John Hollins and Roger Freestone. International signings, in the shape of Matthias Verschave and Nicholas Fabiano, were made too late and the free transfer of David Romo, also from France, showed a leaning towards agents and foreign players that the fans questioned when so many British-born players were on Swansea's doorstep. Again Roger is philosophical on the lack of transfer activity at the club and the team's subsequent reversal of fortunes, 'I don't know why we never signed anybody, I really don't. I'm not privy to that information, I just hear what everyone else hears, but I do form my own opinions, you do that as you get older and maybe a bit wiser. It was obvious to me that we needed a few good players in the squad, and everyone expected it, especially when you read quotes from the manager and Mike Lewis that this was going to happen. Mark Stein was one target I knew about, but that fell apart – probably a good thing for us when you see his performances for Luton. He was someone who the manager knew from Chelsea, so it didn't come as a surprise to me that Stein was being mentioned, but he wasn't the answer as far as I was concerned. Mark Robins was another who Steve Hamer was keen on, but he went to Rotherham, and what a contrast in fortunes between us and them after the season before. It was frustrating, but we just worked as hard as we could with John Hollins and hoped for the best.'

'Yes it was getting rather inevitable towards the end that we would go straight back down, but we are professionals and we clung on to the hope that we would get it right. I think it all went wrong when we drew at Swindon, after that there was a sense of doom and gloom. Then we lost at Colchester, and I made some real schoolboy errors that cost us the game. The manager was not at all complimentary towards me after that – you could see he was under pressure and he blamed me for the team's relegation that season, which I thought was a bit harsh. I didn't think I was to blame for everything; okay, I had made a bad mistake or two that night, and at Walsall when we lost 5-1, but to blame me for everything was a bit naughty. But he was under pressure, and I took what he said on board. He didn't have to say it but he did. Maybe I was right to sign that contract after all, or maybe I would have been transfer listed too.'

Hollins' outburst against Roger followed taunts from the Swansea City fans towards the manager. Swansea's support still travelled in decent numbers throughout the season, and they were demanding a change in fortune. As he says, Roger was probably lucky to have signed the contract extension a few months before, giving him some security as things began to go wrong at the club. Roger had spent a few months in discussions with the club and seemed to be getting nowhere when he approached Mike Lewis to sort it out. 'I just wanted to sign and get it out of the way. I was getting annoyed with the manager because he was fobbing me off all the time, and it got to a stage where I was ignoring the man, he was making me angry. So I went and sorted it out with Lewis. In the end I agreed to the terms they offered and I wanted to stay at the club so I signed. The shock for me was when Lewis asked me about the signing-on fee. He then offered me a decent wedge to sign on again, and I left his office in a bit of a dither. It was the last thing I expected from him, to be offered money for extending my contract. I had just received a signing-on fee the month before this, but he put it in, and I took it gladly. I think that was a mistake on his part, he came to the club as a commercial manager of sorts, having been a programme editor with Fulham, now he was discussing contracts with professional footballers – but he was the general manager, so who was I to argue with him? Suffice to say that Sue and I have now redecorated the house, with new flooring and furniture, and I would like to thank Mike Lewis personally for that.'

The BBC-sponsored FA of Wales Premier Cup gave a brief respite from the relegation campaign, as did the Autowindscreen Trophy. In the FAW Cup Swansea battled their way to a final with Wrexham at The Vetch after hard ties against Carmarthen and Llanelli. Roger was frequently left out of the cup side, and Jason Jones, his understudy, got some games under his belt, although Roger played in the semi-final and final.

In the Autowindscreen Trophy, Swansea players and fans fantasised about a Millennium Stadium appearance, to rub the noses of their near neighbours into the ground for the first time in a couple of years. It was not to be, as Brentford stole a quarter-final away win at The Vetch in extra time. Roger would rather forget the Brentford game, 'Susan came down with the children and a family friend. I was sent off for the first time in my career and was very embarrassed about it. It was for a tackle outside the area, and for my wife and son to see my first sending off ever was humiliating. But I deserved it, I just can't play outfield!' The sending off brought about a return to the first team for Jason Jones, a patient understudy to the normally ever-present Freestone. However, Jones' was sent off, at Bury, leaving Alex Davies to make his debut between the sticks. Roger remembers the club's junior 'keeper with some concern, 'Poor Alex was terrified, he was shaking so much when he went on that Glan Letheran had to hold his hands still to get his gloves on. And then the lad went and saved the penalty with his first touch in League football. But the ref made them take it again, and they scored. That was some introduction for Alex, and I was concerned that the club let him go on a free at the end of the season – he looked very useful at times, even on a par with Jason I thought. I think that move had more to do with saving money and cutbacks than keeping talent.'

As it dawned on the Vetch administration that the club was doomed to another season back in Division Three, they began to offload players and reap the reward for discovering young talent in the Swansea area. Two young hopefuls ended up at Southampton for £200,000, and Roger's closest friend at the club, Steve Jones, was released by Hollins. Steve remembers the day vividly, 'I was stunned. I thought we would be discussing my new contract, instead he released me, which made me really angry. I had literally spilt blood for the club and I felt really let down. You would have thought that even John Hollins could see who wanted to play for Swansea and who didn't, but he couldn't, and players like me and Martin Thomas were let go.' Jones is now engaged in a two-year contract at Cheltenham Town, a club where he played football before they entered the League, and his commitment will not be lost on their manager, Steve Cotterill. Jones is philosophical about the way things worked out, 'In a way Hollins did me a favour by releasing me. My family are my first consideration and even though I didn't mind travelling to Swansea from Gloucestershire every day for training, I now have more time with the people who matter most.' Jones remembers his time with Swansea fondly and will not forget people like

Alan Curtis and Roger Freestone, his best friend in football

Julian Alsop, another former colleague of Roger's, will always be a Swansea follower – in his own words 'It affects you, the whole place is mental, and when the North Bank is on song there's no place like it.' Even after leaving the club, Julian was seen at home games with his old team mates, while friends of the big striker, who once travelled only to see him play, now watch the Swans, as they too have caught the bug. Julian watched with dismay as the side slipped towards relegation and felt for Roger especially. 'Roger is special, a real players' player. He didn't deserve to be a part of that appalling set up that saw Swansea relegated. I couldn't believe it – why did the manager not sign a single player when the club were looking at the Second Division? What the hell was he up to? Roger is as big a Swans nut as anyone, he lives and breaths the place, and he just did not deserve that after pledging himself to the club for so long. I am away from the place now, and to be honest as long as I can play football I am happy, but Swansea City's results are always on my mind, and I long to see them do well. For Roger's sake I hope they do, but nobody at that club who has taken it downwards in the last season or two deserves to be even mentioned alongside Roger. It just wouldn't be right. And the fans have shown massive support for John Hollins – in return he just banned us, the players, from speaking to anyone at all like the fans fanzines and such, and well, I've never known anything like it before. If he was manager anywhere else he would have been booted out.' Of course those words from Julian Alsop were shown to be prophetic upon Hollins' dismissal in September 2001.

Matthew Bound is another Swans player who took relegation hard – 'I know we didn't do ourselves justice, and you don't have to tell me that, but I take the blame for that and I am big enough to know that we can put it right in the future. When I came to Swansea the immediate thing that struck me was the atmosphere with the fans, and I have been lucky to have a good rapport with them since I signed. It may be frowned on by a few people here, but I couldn't care less – what I do in my spare time is my business. Much the same as Roger, I won't be told what I can and cannot do because someone else doesn't like it. I don't bring the club in to any disrepute, and I like a lot of the fans, who have become my friends.' Matthew Bound clearly had a lot of respect for his goalkeeper, 'Roger is the same, he has his own circle of friends away from football, real people who you can rely on – and they know who they are – and really footballers need that, people to talk to and trust, we all do, and no one should tell you who you can and can't talk to and be mates with. Roger was one of the first people I met at the club, he was a noisy bloke sat in the dressing room, making all the jokes and taking the piss generally. But squads need that, and he is a real joker, a right wind up, always messing about and having a laugh, playing tricks and stuff. Once he wound up Steve Jones big time. He was rooming with him, they nearly always did on away trips, and Jonah had fallen asleep. Roger crapped on a piece of paper and put it next to his head while he was sleeping and went to bed. Roger was calling Jonah's name, and woke him up. Jonah turned round to come face to face with this huge turd staring at him, now what a pleasant surprise that must have been! But that's Roger, always larking about and having a laugh. He puts odd things in sandwiches, phones you and makes stuff up, pretending to be an agent from Villa or someone – it's obvious the trip from Newport each day gets his mind racing. But you also know that he cares about his family and would rather be with them than on the piss every day. He talks about DIY and his kids, so clearly there is a good and sane side to him too.'

The greatest testimony to Roger's heart being as big as his goal area came when he won the fans' choice as Goalkeeper of the Year for the 1999/2000 season. Bigsave.com awarded him a cash prize of £3,000, which he gave to the Royal Gwent hospital to be used on their eczema research wing because a young boy next door to Roger in Risca was suffering from an extreme case of the illness. Ryan Crandon, himself a huge football fan, was pictured with Roger in the local paper – a nice story in a somewhat cynical time when £50,000 a week is not enough for some professional footballers.

Among the football heartache of relegation came real heartache for the club, and indeed Roger, when Marlene, a stalwart in the club shop, died. Her friend and long-time colleague, Myra, was devastated. Having just buried her forty-six year old son, who had succumbed to cancer, she had to face up to another loss in a short space of time. Fans of Swansea City know Myra – she is the kind of person that all clubs need. Myra and Marlene have done more for Swansea's cause than any board member or manager could claim to have done. The two women answered the phones, arranged tickets for fans, posted club shop merchandise across the world and, without being asked, spend many hours of their own time at the club for no financial reward. For most Swans fans, they are the spirit of the club.

Myra takes promotion, relegation and the ever-changing squad in her stride. She has seen it all before, but can talk for hours on Roger Freestone. 'I didn't resent Roger when he came to us, but I have always had a thing with goal-keepers' she laughs. 'I was very friendly with Lee Bracey, and Roger replaced him in goal, and for a long time I gave lodgings to Ben Miles, another goalie who came from London way. Jason Price was another lovely boy, he was from Aberdare – not a goalie, but always helping out in the club shop. Roger and Jason would come in and talk to us. Roger was always after a piece of toast and a cup of tea. Back then we had a corner of the shop that was out of the way like, you couldn't see in. Roger and Jason would hide away in there for hours sometimes. If there was a game or a meeting they wouldn't sneak off, they would just come and see us and have a chat and wait. In time Roger served in the club shop, and the supporters liked that a lot, seeing Roger helping out and talking to them sort of made him human in their eyes. And Marlene loved him, she really did like Roger a lot. He was a joker, and you had to keep your eye on him a bit, but he was such a nice person to us, and you get to know the nice ones. Some players have been nothing but prima donnas and rude, but we have been lucky to have Roger at Swansea for so long.'

No matter how nice the people are, no matter how sad the personal losses and no matter what the causes were – Swansea were relegated. Even a 6-0 thrashing of Brentford at the end of the season couldn't change the fact that, for 46 games, Swansea City never really hit it off with Division Two. They toyed with the idea for a while, and at one stage even threatened to stay up, but at the end of it all they were down.

Swansea City have now changed ownership and are looking to get back out of the basement and overtake their South Wales rivals, Cardiff City. The final word on the club's relegation, coming at the end of his tenth season, must go to Roger: 'I was gutted, and like many players I ran my mind through the games and the defeats. And I kept coming back to John Hollins blaming me for our relegation. Even though it wasn't all my fault I take the blame for us losing the important games, and the games that ended up with us losing by the odd goal. Because if it wasn't for me that goal would not have gone in, so being a 'keeper you take it personally, but we didn't strengthen, and the players we brought in like Gio and Verschave and Fabiano were not the answer. They may have been if they had come sooner, but even players of their quality were not good enough to save us. But after a while you get used to the idea, and just thank God you can still play, and at least we can put it right and give the fans something to be proud of. Of all the seasons I have played the 2000/2001 season was my most disappointing. I really thought we had it sorted out, and even though we didn't set the transfer world alight I thought we could do something.

'The fact we didn't after promising so much is, and will always be, very hard to take. Swansea City could have set a base for better and brighter things. We were taking thousands away from home and getting more than break-even crowds at home, but the owners refusal to invest and build from that platform. We started off with 8,500 for the first home game and could have got bigger crowds than that all season, but the owners wanted it on the cheap, that's now apparent. They are to blame as much as the players, the manager and anyone else, and if the truth be known they are the real reason why we failed. We didn't have their support, and the manager didn't have their support, so what did they expect? The money tree was not there, but John Hollins with their support could have done more, and that's the sickening thing. Had they supported him properly instead of wild talk about 25,000 all-seater stadiums we may have stayed up. If Swansea fans want to start any witch hunt they should start with the owners and work from there.' The relegation eventually led to John Hollins leaving the club, which upset Roger, but he concedes that his time was up, and the time to go was right.

13

PLAYING FOR WALES

Roger Freestone has been capped for his country at nearly every level. Schoolboy, youth, under-21 and full international. This chapter reflects those phases and his major influences. For Roger, it was easy come, easy go – for Wales it was an era when he was the nearly man of Welsh football. All speculation regarding Roger's international potential culminated in one hell of a full international debut against the Brazilians at the new Millennium stadium.

'I was thirteen when I first got a taste of international football. To be honest I probably didn't appreciate it that much. I was a typical lad of the time; I loved Madness and all the ska music, and was equally at home with my mates testing out the clobber we wore and the latest Specials single as wearing a football strip for my country. I always wore a green Harrington jacket and had ten-high Doctor Martens boots – that was the uniform of the day for me and my mates. We all had short hair and looked right states I should imagine, but we thought we were the business around Risca. My dad took me for my first Welsh trial at Abergavenny. It was a Sunday, and I did okay, so much so that I was invited along to real training at Sophia Gardens in Cardiff. A lot of the lads were two years older than me, but I didn't feel out of place. Chris Whitley was the man in overall charge of us and he was a great man I thought. He commanded a lot of respect from the boys in the squad, but he was very fair. I looked up to him a lot. Another lad, Wayne Russell, was playing for Wales at the time, he was a remarkable player and someone who stood out for his country above the rest. I spent two years with that squad under the guidance of Chris. It was a great time, but as I have already said it was indeed something I took for granted. I rarely had any nerves, but I would get those at a later stage of my career!

It was quite disciplined, and I suppose it had to be with all these young lads – some with big egos – running about. I was lucky to have played for Gwent schools at under-11 and under-13 level, which was the reason why I had been picked for Wales, and of course I was lucky that I lived in the right area of Wales too. It didn't make me any different to me as a person though, all my mates at the time – Steve Thomas, Chris James, Paul John, Chris Hannan and loads more – were more interested in bouncing around to *Baggy Trousers* than anything else. I was looking at being a professional footballer and I suppose they just accepted it. We would meet in our youth club at Rogerstone Primary as it was then – they had converted the old kitchen into a youth club which we all went to on Tuesdays and Thursdays. That was a great time to be young I thought. Playing records and discovering girls, the sort of thing I suppose all young boys get into and lose any chance of being a professional player. But I had one eye on the girls and one eye on the football: I thought for a lad of such a young age I was pretty sorted really.

'I was selected for the under-15 squad when we played at Tynecastle in Edinburgh against Scotland. I didn't get on but it was a great experience travelling away with the players, and it seemed so far away. Then it all happened at once. I was picked and played against the Republic of Ireland at Abertillery, we drew that 3-3. Then I played against England, Scotland and Northern Ireland too. Whilst all this was going on I was playing on weekends, and getting games for Newport Schools and of course Gwent Schools too. It was football, football, football – and I loved it. To cap it all I heard that Manchester United wanted me, but my dad didn't pursue it – maybe he didn't want me to leave, maybe he wanted to be able to keep an eye on me, and anyway I had Newport County interested too!

'The first two years at under-15 level were great. We played no end of games and the highlight had to be playing against Germany. We lost both games 2-0 and 5-0 respectively, but it was a great experience. Then it was time to move on up a level and that was a great time too. I was selected for the under-18 squad in January 1985 and made my debut in a 3-0 win against Northern Ireland at The Racecourse. I remember Iwan Roberts playing, and the manager then was one Mike England. He was not a bad bloke, and seemed at home coaching young players. Some managers are happier with youngsters than with seasoned pros – a bit like John Hollins at Swansea, they seem to get the best out of youngsters and enjoy the rewards. At seventeen I was a Welsh regular and I was also at Newport County.

'Mike England rewarded me for my endeavour by picking me for the European Championship squad and Newport County loaned me out for trial at Watford with Graham Taylor. He was a really nice man, and you could see he was a real football man. He wasn't unpleasant and rude like some, he was genuinely interested and happy to have us there. We stayed with a life-long Watford fan in the town. He was a Greek guy and Watford mad. But after a week we came home again. Graham spoke to us when we left, he wished us well, and I didn't feel let down or anything. The last thing on my mind was to sign for Watford, and Darren [Peacock] was the same. I wanted to be involved with the Wales squad more than anything. The European Championships were a bit of a let down too. We played at the Heysel Stadium against Belgium and lost 2-0 and then went to Holland and played them in Amsterdam. We just missed out on qualification, which was a gutter but it gave me a real taste of things to come and untold experience of playing with players – in fact the very best players in Europe at my age. I went on to play for the under-21 side against Poland at Pennydarren Park, we won that 2-0. But that side was not a cash winner for the Welsh FA and under-21 sides at that time were not a great idea. But it did introduce players like myself, Andy Melville and Chelsea's Gareth Hall to international football, and it doesn't matter what level you play at, when you are taking on the best around it has to do you good.

'Mike Smith was the under-21 manager, and he was the man who picked me for my first full squad in 1995. It was as third choice, but initially I didn't care, it was just great to be there. But of course you want to progress, and under Mike Smith that clearly was not going to happen for me. He was picking Neville Southall as number one – which was fine, that went without saying – but what really annoyed me was that he never gave me the chance as a number two. He would pick Tony Roberts, who was QPR number two, and I just couldn't get a look in. But the players were fantastic. I was rubbing shoulders with the likes of Ryan Giggs, Ian Rush, Mark Hughes, Dean Saunders – some real household names. I was in my element, and then Vinny Jones came along!

'Vinny is magic and a complete headbanger. He was a real breath of fresh air for the Welsh squad. He loved it and took on the role big time. We played against Georgia, and God knows what they made of him – he was a permanent wind-up to those lads. He had the feathers tattooed on his leg, and learned the Welsh National Anthem. He was inspiring and great to be around. He has gone on to do some amazing things with his career, and it is no surprise at all. He came too late for Wales and should have been involved from the earliest opportunity. I know he has his fans and he has his critics, but Vinny was more than a hard midfield player, he was inspiring and a real motivator. He had charisma falling out of his ears, and I don't care what anyone says, he was a real footballers' footballer, a class act and a genuine person. You knew what you got with Vinny, he hid nothing, and the world would be a better place if more were like him. Maybe that's why some folk didn't like him, he was honest. Of course that trait in a person is not liked if you are the opposite, I will say no more.

'In the end though, Wales did get to see me play at full international level, and that for me was the biggest day in my sporting life.'

The records show a vast number of Welsh appearances for Roger Freestone. Furthermore, his desire to play and remain in Wales makes it surprising that he has not represented his country far more at full international level. The quality he showed at a young age, which saw rave reviews when on international duty, has always been there. But for a number of Welsh managers, the fact he was at Swansea City in the lower divisions of the Football League was a problem.

Roger will always reflect on this, but knows that his life away from football is more important than life in it. His experiences at such a young age in Reading with Sue always push themselves to the front of his mind whenever his professional career is spoken about. Although the Premiership bias of previous managers of the national side have held him back, in Roger's opinion Wales has not seen the best of him.

The authors of this book would certainly agree with this – never mind the level, look at the quality! When Garry Lloyd, the Barry Town full-back, was selected for the national side, Roger felt some resentment that a player in the League of Wales would deserve attention from Bobby Gould when someone with a good reputation in League football did not. Perhaps Roger plies his trade too far west of the Welsh capital to be worthy of a place – indeed, when second choice Cardiff City goal-keeper Pat Mountain was called up, Roger must have wondered what he had to do to attract the attention of the Welsh management. Despite such possible political influences or oversights of the management, Roger would be the first to accept that, when on top of his game, Neville Southall was always number one as far as his country was concerned.

Roger knows he owes Mark Hughes much for his bravery in picking him while playing for in a newly promoted Division Two side – that selection has cemented Roger Freestone's place in the game he loves, and in the history of the national side he has represented at nearly every level since the age of thirteen.

A rare sight: Roger is beaten as England score against Wales under-15s.

Left: Aged fourteen and an under-15 international. Right: Proudly wearing the red jersey of Wales.

Roger with fellow under-15 team mates Jamie King (left) and Sean Wharton.

The Welsh squad that faced the Republic of Ireland in 1983.

Training with the full Welsh squad before being selected for his full international debut against Brazil.

14

THE FUTURE
BY ROGER FREESTONE

'Fifteen and a half years as a professional footballer is more than I could have ever hoped for and I am grateful for what the game has given me. It must be every schoolboy's dream to play football professionally, and for me that dream came true. When I look back over the years there are so many happy memories. Wembley wins, the biggest stadia in the land, triumph and of course international caps are some of the things that come to mind straightaway. Of course, as well as the highs there have been some lows and some games that hurt for a long time after we lost them. Talking to Keith and Phil as they put this book together sent me off on so many journeys through my memory bank it was untrue. There are some things that will have happened to people that you will not automatically remember but when you start digging into the past, there are things that you come across that you wonder how you ever forgot.

'I have to say that when I signed professional terms at Newport County, I never believed that I would still be here now. When you are seventeen you make no rash predictions of what you will be doing when you are thirty-three. This game has given me so much and one of the things that I would like to make sure happens is that when I finally decide enough is enough that I give something back. I would like to go into coaching, I started studying for my exams on this front a while back, but have to admit that this is something that I have let go in recent times. I will rectify this over the coming years and, who knows, maybe in ten years time you may be reading about Roger Freestone, goalkeeping coach extraordinaire! Having said that, I have no idea on when I want to give up the playing side of the game. At thirty-three, I still have two years remaining on my current contract. After that I would like at least one more renewal, but that is purely dependent on my physical condition at the time and whether I feature in the manager's plans for the future. Football can be a fickle profession – which is why I believe that you should take one day at a time and never make promises that you cannot guarantee can come true. Whatever happens, I would like to stay in football as long as I possibly can. It is a great sport and for me, it just happens to be the best job that I could have had. Funny people may say that it is the only job I could have had and to a degree that is true but, whatever, I feel privileged to have played the game.

'Sometimes I have to pinch myself to realise that I have been at Swansea for ten years now. I can still remember vividly the day that I signed and playing against Tottenham at the Vetch on the same day. When I put pen to paper I would never have predicted that ten years later I would still be there. And from my point of view, it's not just the ten years, it's also the fact that I have played first-team football for all that time. And through all that time, the fans have been so good to me; they have wherever I have played in truth. Swansea is such a great place to play football. I love the club and it is, literally, my second home. The club is one where there aren't dull days. Very rarely do you find us in a comfortable mid-table position. I remember so many people telling me that it's a rollercoaster ride and, if that's true, then there can't be too many rollercoasters as enjoyable as Swansea.

'How about management? I would love to be a football manager, but whether I can be, or indeed will be, is a different matter. If you take the number of people that play football professionally and the number that get into management then that proves just how hard it is. Sure, I would love to give it a stab, but I would rather be thought of as a good goalkeeper rather than a poor football manager so we will have to see. There are better players than me who have never made it, but sometimes with these things it's being in the right place at the right time. All I do know is that if the chance did ever come up in the future then I would grab it with both hands (safe hands I hope you are saying!) and give it the best shot that I could.

'Picking out the best moment from my career is a nigh on impossible task. I am very proud of all the medals that I have won, right up from my schoolboy records through to the championship medal that I won in 2000. Winning my first cap was one of the proudest moments of my career and one of the things that you always aim for. Once I passed thirty I believed that maybe the chance had gone, but they do say that goalkeepers get better with age. Individual matches or moments are nigh on impossible to pick out and say "that was the best" and I'm not sure if the book publishers will give me enough space to write about them all! One of the big highlights for me is playing first-team football for the last ten years. That is all I really wanted when I signed terms was to play football again. The last couple of years at Chelsea showed me that I needed to play football. That is what I think I am good at, and for me to be able to do it constantly over that period is a big honour. Football has bought me so much pleasure and I like to think that people get pleasure out of watching me play. It was also a great honour to be awarded a testimonial season by Swansea City. I hope to be able to sit down this time next year and look over the year and reflect on how good it was. But, of course it goes without saying that it will only be a success in my mind off the pitch providing it is on the pitch at the same time.

'I have never been one to set myself goals and ambitions and to sit down and think about if I have anything unfulfilled in the game was a very difficult task. Short term, my main ambition is to get Swansea promoted back to Division Two. Relegation that season was painful and this football club should not be in Division Three. If I can play my part in any promotion success then I will be very happy indeed. Last season I made my 500th League appearance, which was a very special day for me, and even more so as I managed to celebrate the landmark with a clean sheet. There are a couple of big landmarks for me that I think are in my sight. At the end of the 2001 season, I had made 549 appearances for the club in all competitions. I believe that the club record is held by Wilf Milne, who made 657 appearances. With luck, I can break that record – which would be a massive milestone when you think of some of the names that have passed through this club during its history. Wilf I am told also made 585 League appearances. I have 453 at the moment for the club, so maybe I have that record in my sights as well? It's ironic, the number of League games I have played for the club as I could, in theory, open next season with my 500th League appearance in a Swansea City shirt, now that would be a way to celebrate.

There are so many people within the game that I would like to thank for my career. I apologise to anyone that I miss out but, as with so many things, there are just too many too mention. The first is possibly the most obvious, all the managers that have given me contracts. It goes without saying that without those people, ranging from Colin Addison, who offered my first contract at Newport through to John Hollins who offered me the new deal I signed last season, my career would have been very different. All these managers have shown faith in my ability – without them, who knows what I would be doing these days. A special word of thanks must go to Glan Letheran, who has taken my career to a new level since he started coaching me. I have no doubt that I would have not played for Wales had it not been for Glan and I will always be grateful to him for that. I don't believe it's any coincidence that the record I set for clean sheets in our championship season was done under the watchful eye of Glan and I hope that if I do make it into coaching then I can be at least half the coach he is. I also owe a big debt of gratitude to Frank Burrows. Frank rescued me from Chelsea at a time when my career was going nowhere and if it wasn't for him then the last ten years would have been completely different. I imagine that you wouldn't be sitting reading this book if it wasn't for him and there is nothing I can say or do to repay him for what he did for me. Mark Hughes also deserves a special mention for my Welsh cap. It is refreshing to know that playing in the lower divisions counts for nothing as far as "Sparky" is concerned, and I am grateful to him for putting me on the biggest stage that there is.

'There is a group of people that I haven't yet thanked, but they are the most important people in my life – my family. From the very start of my career they have been right behind me and supportive in what I have done. It hasn't always been easy, particularly for Sue, but she has always been there and I don't know what I would have done without her. Sue has been part of my life for as long as I can remember, we have been married now for thirteen years and they have been great years. We are lucky enough to have two wonderful children in Dan and Lauren and it has been a complete joy watching them grow up. Being a footballer means that I am away from home quite a bit and credit has to go to Sue for the way she has coped with my absence at times, especially at the traditional family time of Christmas. That time of year is something I will look forward to if I am ever outside football – a normal Christmas where I can have a few more glasses of sherry! But of course, the children do know what I have to do and I am incredibly proud of both of them. Maybe Dan will follow me into football, but at the end of it if he does or not, he will always have my backing in the same way that my parents did for me.

Sue's parents have always been right behind us as well, and without all these people and other members of my family then I would not be here now and still doing what I love.

'I would also like to thank anyone else that has encouraged, supported and backed me during my time as a professional. There are times that you need all the support that you can get and, without the encouragement, then who knows what might have happened to me. Another thanks goes to you, the fans. There is no better experience as a professional then hearing your fans getting behind you. At times, the noise when I have played has been almost as good as a goal start and football would not be there if it wasn't for you people. I hope you have got as much out of my career as I have and I hope that you continue to do so as I reach my twilight years.

'Finally, a thanks to Keith and Phil who have spent so much time with me over the past year writing this book. I hope that you have found my story interesting and enjoyed an insight into life as a professional footballer. I think the Swansea City story fits in well with mine. I cannot profess to Champions League or World Cup medals, but I have always given everything I have when I have played, and as I start my testimonial season I still view every day as another day at the office.'

AFTERWORD

During the completion of this book, Swansea City Football Club changed hands on two further occasions. Initially, Neil McClure and his company devolved their basic interests to Mike Lewis. In the three months leading to October 2001, Tony Petty became the new chairman and, apparently, the owner. Mike Lewis, although no longer involved at the club, still attended games as Petty attempted to dispose of the services of Steve Watkin, John Williams, Jason Smith, Matthew Bound, David Romo and Nicholas Mezzina. Another seven players, including Roger Freestone, were told that their contracts were to be drastically reduced.

As this book was completed, the fate of Swansea City Football Club still hung in the balance. We can only hope that Roger and the Swans fans get the leadership they deserve, so Roger can keep spending another day at the office for the club that he loves.

STATISTICS

Full Name: Roger Freestone

Family: Wife: Sue (married 18 June 1988)
Children: Daniel Leigh (born 30 August 1990),
Lauren Michelle (born 10 December 1992)

Home: Risca

Place Of Birth: Newport

Clubs: Newport County
Chelsea
Swansea City (Loan)
Hereford United (Loan)
Swansea City

Moves: Trainee - Newport County 2 April 1986
Newport County - Chelsea 10 March 1987
Chelsea - Swansea City (Loan) 29 September 1989
Chelsea - Hereford United (Loan) 9 March 1990
Chelsea - Swansea City 5 September 1991

League Appearances:
Newport County - 13
Chelsea - 42
Swansea (Loan) - 14
Hereford (Loan) - 8
Swansea City - 439
Total League Appearances - 516

Cup Appearances:
Newport County - 1
Chelsea - 11
Swansea (Loan) - 1
Hereford (Loan) - 0
Swansea City - 95
Total Cup Appearances - 108

Total Appearances:

        Newport County - 14
        Chelsea - 53
        Swansea (Loan) - 15
        Hereford (Loan) - 8
        Swansea City - 534
        Total Appearances - 624

Goals:

        Swansea City - 3 League goals

Honours:

        Second Division Championship 1989
        Third Division Championship 2000
        Autoglass Trophy 1994
        1 Full Welsh Cap
        1 under-21 Cap
        Youth honours, under-15

Career statistics are correct to the end of the 2000/2001 season.